Ian Carroll is a best selling author,
Amazon in paperback and also on Kin

G000060725

Ian is the author of the 'A-Z of Blc
among its titles – *'Warning: Water N
Shop', 'Clown in Aisle 3' and 'Pensic*
books *'My Name is Ishmael', ᴅemon Pirates Vs. Vikings –
Blackhorn's Revenge', 'The Lover's Guide to Internet Dating'* and
'Valentines Day'.
Ian is also the author of many Music Books including the *'Fans Have
Their Say'* series and Official Book of the Reading Festival (UK). Plus
the Books on the 'Saving the Reel Cinema' campaign.

Ian lives with his wife Raine, two sons – Nathan & Josh - plus Stanley
and the memories of a jet-black witches cat called Rex - in Plymouth,
Devon, UK.

Paddy is a 41-year-old author/singer/songwriter, who has a passion for
writing, and whose weapon of choice is clearly the pen.

Paddy hails from Dublin, but is firmly rooted here in Plymouth.
He has five children, Regan, Shauna, Lilianna, Coby and Freya, which
keeps him on his toes.

He is the author of *'Plymouth, a War in Words'*, which is dedicated to
the history of the 'Ocean City' in which he resides. Paddy is an avid
writer of all things poetical and macabre and has many poems and short
stories published to his name.
Paddy's mind is a mesh of King, Herbert and Koontz all rolled into one
big ball of horrific fiction and is compelled to give anybody a scare.

Carroll and Mullen, the new names in Horror & Local History

ISBN - 9798669139308

2020

The Year We Did Nothing –
Plymouth a City Under Lockdown

© Ian Carroll & Paddy Mullen 2020

2020 the Year We Did Nothing…

A New Decade.

New hopes, new ideas, new plans - but no one had planned for what was about to happen in Plymouth and all around the world from only a few months into the start of the New Year.

Plymouth Argyle were flying high in League Two with their aspirations set on winning the league and getting promoted to League One, only 1 point off the League leaders Swindon Town and Crewe on equal points with Swindon, only lagging behind on goal difference.

Outdoor concerts had been booked and subsequently sold out for Westlife and Little Mix at Home Park (Plymouth Argyle's stadium) and Tom Jones on Plymouth Hoe.

The preparations were all completed and everything was set for the celebrations in Plymouth, throughout the year for Mayflower 400 - 'an amazing year of events in 2020 commemorating the Journey of the Mayflower'.

Concerts and comedy shows were confirmed at the Plymouth Pavilions and further afield a stellar line-up was booked for the 'Eden Sessions' at St. Austell's environmentally friendly Eden Project.

Further away, all across the country, festivals had been arranged and were selling well or tickets had already sold out for Download Festival, Glastonbury Festival, Beautiful Days, Reading Festival and hundreds more including the first Weekender dance festival at Newnham Park in Plympton on the outskirts of Plymouth.

Theatre productions were booked solid at the Theatre Royal with many shows completely booked up for the whole year.

The Euro 2020 football competition was on the horizon, with hopes of another, if not more successful campaign from the still relatively young England squad.

Wimbledon was being prepared for with tickets sold and people looking ahead with anticipation to their Pimms and strawberries & cream in the sun and perhaps another British youngster coming up through the ranks.

The 2020 Olympics in Japan were to be a highlight of the summers sporting calendar, with athletics, tennis, football, swimming and more to look forward too.

And then it all went wrong...

The news began to report on a virus -which gradually became an epidemic in China - COVID-19. The WHO (World Health Organisation) reported in January 2020 on a Coronavirus epidemic, beginning to spread from Wuhan City in the Hubei Province of China. Initially thought not to be as deadly as the SARS epidemic in 2003, it was soon realised that its transmission rate was significantly higher and the death toll began to rise.

And then it hit Europe...

Italy was the first to suffer badly from the spread of COVID-19 and then the cases began to slowly occur in the UK at the beginning of February.

By 5th March, the UK had its first COVID-19 related death and with a steady increase, by 31st March the death toll had reached 3095; the UK was part of the first 'pandemic' that nearly anyone had experienced in his or her lifetime and the country was put into 'Lock-Down'.

Only essential shops, chemists, petrol stations were open and the only people allowed to go to work were 'key workers' - NHS staff, police, teachers, Civil Servants, essential shop workers - the city of Plymouth was a 'ghost town' with nothing before seen like it in our lives.

As the death toll rose, that was all that was covered on the news - SKY News, BBC news, ITV news were wall to wall pandemic coverage, with only a brief respite with the VE Day celebrations, to commemorate the 75th Anniversary, with everything still done at a 2 metre 'social distancing' – and 'Captain Tom' Moore walking laps of his garden to raise money for the NHS to help during the crisis; after successfully raising over £32 million, Captain Tom was made an Honorary Colonel and knighted to become Captain Sir Thomas Moore, a slight and rare ray of hope in amongst all the anguish and heartache.

The amount of deaths per day eventually began to plateau, though face masks on public transport and social distancing was still 'a thing' even as some of the previous months strict rules were relaxed, with non-essential shops reopening and a slight return to normality is occurring each week.

30th April - 27,510 Dead
31st May - 39,045 Dead
17th June - 42,288 Dead

Plymouth Argyle were promoted to League One when the remaining games were decided not to be played and Exeter entered the 'play offs' and secured their place at Wembley Stadium in London for the 'League Two Play Off Final' to also try and win promotion to the League above. The Premier League and the Championship came back - but behind closed doors.

But the wait for Theatre shows, concerts and festivals might have to wait until 2021.

So, there we have it. 2020, a year like no other, one where we made new friends and spoke to our neighbours, clapped for the NHS and seemed to queue with no problems as that's what the British do best!!

This Book will act as a memory to pass down to your children and grandchildren, of what we didn't do in 2020.

Ian Carroll (Plymouth) June 2020

Ian Carroll prepares for his first trip – with facemask – on the bus home.

Coronavirus Timeline

31ˢᵗ December – *China alerts the WHO to the new virus that has started to occur in and around the city of Wuhan.*

23ʳᵈ January – *Wuhan is locked down.*

25ᵗʰ January – *The Foreign and Commonwealth Offices advises the UK population not to travel to Wuhan in China or anywhere in Hubei Province due to the outbreak.*

27ᵗʰ January – *200 British citizens in Wuhan are offered repatriation back to the UK, due to the Coronavirus outbreak taking control in the city.*

28ᵗʰ January – *All travel to Mainland China is warned against, bar essential travel.*

31ˢᵗ January – *First two cases of COVID-19 are confirmed as occurring in the UK and NHS England declares the first ever 'Level 4 Critical Incident'.*

11ᵗʰ February – *Case number 9 of COVID-19 is confirmed in the UK*

12ᵗʰ February – *Exeter University warns that if left unchallenged, 45 million people in the UK could easily become infected.*

15ᵗʰ February – *The first Coronavirus death takes place in Europe.*

28ᵗʰ February – *The first British Coronavirus death is confirmed.*

29ᵗʰ February – *NHS management send out warnings about the shortage of PPE.*

3rd March – *The public are advised to no longer shake hands.*

9th March – *Ireland cancels all St. Patrick's Day parades.*

10th March – *Cheltenham Festival continues, with around 250,000 'punters' attending over the 4-day event.*

11th March – *The World Health Organisation declares the COVID-19 outbreak as a 'global pandemic'.*

12th March - *Herd Immunity for the UK is the plan for going forward.*

13th March – *The WHO declares Europe as the epicentre of the pandemic.*

20th March – *UK Pubs and schools close.*

23rd March – *The UK goes into 'Lockdown'.*

26th March – *Both the Download and Isle of Wight Festivals are cancelled due to the pandemic. The first 'Clap for Carers' takes place, with millions of people taking to the streets to clap and show their support for the NHS and other nurses countrywide, from outside their houses.*

27th March – *Both Boris Johnson and his aide Dominic Cummings are both confirmed to have Coronavirus.*

29th March - *The first NHS nurse dies from COVID-19.*

1st April – *Contactless payments in shops are raised from £30 to £45 to lessen the cash handling in stores.*

4th April – *Keir Starmer is elected as the new leader of the Labour Party succeeding Jeremy Corbyn. There is no celebration or public show due to the pandemic.*

5th April – Queen Elizabeth II makes a rare TV appearance to address to the nation about the current pandemic paying tribute to the NHS, care workers and all other 'keyworkers'.

6th April – *Boris Johnson is taken into Intensive Care with COVID-19; Dominic Raab steps up as his deputy, to run the country in his absence. National Express cancels all its long distance coach services.*

11th April – *The Queen addresses the nation with an Easter speech for the first time ever.*

12th April - *UK death toll hits 10,000.*

14th April – *Reports of more arson attacks on mobile phone masts are reported on the news, having occurred over the weekend.*

16th April – *Captain Tom Moore, WWII war veteran aged 99, completes 100 laps of his garden for charity – donating all the money to the NHS. The current total for his raised money stands at £32,796,357 (as of 19/07/20).*

25th April – *Official UK death toll is now 20,000.*

22nd April – *Parliament holds its very first Prime Ministers questions 'Virtually'.*

23rd April – *BBC has the 'Big Night In' fundraiser, which amasses £27 million for charitable causes.*

24th April – *Michael Ball and Captain Tom Moore hit #1 on the charts with their version of the classic 'You'll Never Walk Alone', with money accumulated going to NHS charities.*

27th April – Families of NHS and care workers are told that they will get a payment of £60,000 if their relative who works in the care profession dies of COVID-19.

28th April – *The country hold a 'minute's silence' to remember all the people who have died during the pandemic so far.*

30th April – *Captain Tom Moore celebrates his 100th Birthday in 'lock-down' and is made an honorary Colonel by her majesty the Queen.*

1st May – *Controversial 'celebrity' David Icke has his Facebook account deleted for spreading 'misinformation.*

6th May – *Death toll in the UK goes over 30,000.*

7th May – *PPE gowns (400,000 in total) imported from Turkey are deemed to have failed to meet health and safety standards and are impounded, not to be used. The Notting Hill Carnival is cancelled.*

12th May – *UK's 'Furlough Scheme' is extended further to October, with employees receiving 80% of their wages whilst they are at home. The Reading and Leeds Festivals are cancelled due to the outbreak; the first time that there hasn't been a Reading Festival since 1985 (and I should know, as I've been 33 times…)*

COVID-19 Alert Level System

5 As level 4 and there is a material risk of healthcare services being overwhelmed.

4 A COVID-19 epidemic is in general circulation; transmission is high or rising exponentially.

3 A COVID-19 epidemic is in general circulation.

2 COVID-19 is present in the UK, but the number of cases and transmission is low.

1 COVID-19 no longer present in the UK.

13th May – *Creamfields Festival is cancelled.*

15th May – *Matt Hancock announces that by the start of June every resident and member of staff in all the UK care homes will be tested for the virus.*

16th May – *Protests and marches start for the Coronavirus in London and Glasgow, not everyone wearing masks or 'social distancing'.*

17th May – *Death toll reaches 34,636.*

18th May – *Chelsea Flower is 'virtual' for the first time ever.*

19th May – *It's announced that Captain Tom Moore will be knighted by the Queen, becoming Captain Sir Thomas Moore.*

23rd May – *It's announced that Dominic Cummings (aid to Boris Johnson) travelled from London to Durham to self-isolate – a 520 mile round trip.*

26th May – *The annual Turner Prize is cancelled due to the outbreak.*

28th May – *Premier League clubs agree to restart live games, with the proposed date being the 17th June to carry on where the 2019/20 left off.*

1st June – *Primary schools and Ikea re-open in England and the first horse racing resumes at Newcastle.*

5th June – *The Death toll reaches 40,261.*

9th June – *League One and League Two football seasons are curtailed with the end of season results finishing as they stand. Plymouth Argyle are promoted in third place, back up to League One after only one season in League Two – proving that they were too good for that league and that Derek Adams appeared to be to blame for the previous seasons relegation.*

15th June – *The Great North Run is cancelled.*

16th June – *More than 600,000 people lost their jobs between the months of March and May it is announced. The Premier League returns on BBC1, Sky, BT Sport, Twitch, Pick and Amazon Prime.*

19th June – *COVID-19 alert is dropped to Level 3, from 4.*

25th June – *A major incident is reported, when during a very hot period people flock to the beaches – especially in Bournemouth – as 500,000 people travel to the Dorset coast.*
Liverpool FC wins the Premier League and Anfield is besieged by celebrating fans.

30th June – *Leicester is put under a stricter 'lockdown' after their cases increase – with the rest of the country more relaxed now.*

4th July – *UK holds another minute's silence for the COVID-19 deaths.*

4th July – *The TV programme 'Panorama' on the BBC reports that many more people will die from cancer, due to there treatments being delayed due to the hospitals caring for COVID-19 patients. Highest estimate being 35,000 deaths.*

13th July – *Boris Johnson warns that people should be wearing facemasks in shops – rulings to follow (from 24th July it will become compulsory to wear the face masks in shops).*

15th July – *VAT cut introduced temporarily for the food industry to help them and get people back in restaurants and takeaways.*

17th July – Captain Tom Moore is knighted by the Queen.

Stay Inside

So here it is, a full lockdown evoked,
half way through and still some folks.
Not sticking to the rules, not sticking to the guide,
in parks and on beaches these people defied.
Stay the feck indoors, this is no fun,
playing Russian roulette as you hold the gun.

Dropping like flies, around a big pile of shit,
While we're all inside, doing our bit.
There's welts on my hands and my head is unkempt,
Three more weeks at least to expect.
So stick to the plan, just play the waiting game,
were all in this together, and we also feeling the strain.

And later down the road, with memories at our back,
We can all look past and ponder, about this COVID attack.
For some they will be raw, for others just a trait,
For life during the virus, decided well our fates.
So do us all a favour, don't be such a dick,
Stay the hell indoors, and stop making people sick.

Paddy 18.04.20

"I entered my 87 year old parents house for the first time in 3 months. They were still social distancing whilst social bickering."
Greg Baser (Plymouth)

"We did different things, learnt new skills and hopefully re-understood what really matters.
Many of us worked our socks off through it all, and still are."
Jill Mansfield (Plymouth)

"I am a person of Plymouth but my lockdown was in Madrid. Imagine what that was like.
Pure zombie hell at first."
Simon Jennings (Plymouth)

"I never thought this would happen in my lifetime."
Carole Dinham (Plymouth)

"Hasn't affected myself as I've been working and my partner who has COPD and diabetes has been taking me to work, so the only thing it's affected is me not seeing my family."
Marsha Griffin (Plymouth)

"Things had started feeling very odd in the run up to lockdown.
The managers out in force restocking toilet roll during the toilet roll panic."
Lily Style (Plymouth)

"The peace and fresh air from the lack of planes, trains and automobiles was one of the most amazing parts of lockdown.
The lack of the White Rabbit syndrome of Alice in Wonderland, with people seemingly more relaxed. People had time to say hello if you was in your front garden.
Nobody seemed to care about queuing, as there was no rush to be somewhere. In fact it was time out.
We got to know our community, more so every Thursday evening. Feeling part of that community was even better. Thinking it was Tuesday and it was Wednesday, which continued with more days getting confused as lockdown continued and that wasn't just me.
Sharing and caring, not seen that for decades.
Oh and well-maintained front gardens, and people recycling more. Generosity of the giver with furloughing. I never got any though.
Best, best of all though fuel dropped to under a £1. Amazing, but nobody needed to use it!!"
Grace Stickland (Plymouth)

GRACE STICKLAND

"I want to bloody forget it! Lol" Stacey 'Ginger Chops' Goff (The Hive Mind Comic Book Shop, Frankfort Gate Plymouth – now open)

"Stay at home we were told.
Don't see anybody outside your household.
So the majority of us did that.
Covid then came and attacked my family. Living at the other end of the city rendered me useless, I couldn't help them, I was climbing the walls.
My emotions were emotional. They were so poorly.
Thankfully they came through it and Covid didn't win. We know how lucky that made them.
So many lives lost and yet today there are so many complacent humans out there that still believe Covid isn't real."
Mandi Hafford (Plymouth)

"For me it's that I have had to continue working, as has my partner and this has been extremely stressful - often we haven't had time to cook or shop and I know I've been running on empty.

We are 12 weeks in and there appears to be no let up on the work front. It'll be interesting to see what happens in the recovery stage - though this has highlighted inequality in society more than anything in recent years. Lots of furloughed workers who will soon be returning to work refreshed from a long period of learning new skills, redecorating their homes and spending more time with their children.

Whereas key workers have worked more than usual, often with no increase in pay and some with organisational changes which will continue to have an impact on them long after this is over.

Key workers will be continuing to work once this has all ended and for me, I would like to find a meaningful way of demonstrating gratitude to teachers, supermarket workers, carers, hospital staff, social workers etc. So yeah - for me lockdown has been about working more, eating less and gaining more gray hairs!"

Elizabeth Ann Cheeseright (Plymouth)

"I went back in time using Alexa. Great to hear the bands from the Dike that you had forgotten, look at old flyers and tell it to play music from these bands, takes you back."
Robert Bickell (Plymouth)

"My most vivid memory of the lockdown is driving to work on near empty roads. It was a hot day and as such I had the roof down on my car. People would stare at me as though I was crazy, although everything felt normal inside of my bubble every glance I took outside made it very apparent the world was in turmoil and fear.
It raised a question with me that stuck with me for a while how can we protect from something we can't see."
Josh Smith (Plymouth)

"Worked all through it so hasn't made that much difference."
Steven Moore (Plymouth)

"Eight weeks into an illness.. still haven't seen a doctor!
Still waiting on a CT scan.. let's hope it's not serious.
Can someone now wake the NHS up?"
Karen Gadd (Plymouth)

L	ong hair	**L**	oneliness
O	utbreak	**I**	solation
C	aptain Tom	**F**	urlough
K	eyworkers	**E**	ducating
D	aily updates		at home
O	nline shopping		
W	orking from home		
N	HS		

Kate Fewson-Shanahan (Plymouth)

"I miss lockdown."
Justin Kelso (Plymouth)

For All to Breath

Smoking Woodbines, e-cigarettes,
Coughs a plenty and noses wet,
Sharing fag butts, dirty feckers,
Bus's empty double-deckers.

Kids in park, dirty finger,
Wash your hands, don't let it linger.
Drinking cans, lager stale,
No common sense, will they prevail?

Scratching arse crack, wipe on sleeve,
Spreading germs, on handles, leave.
This pandemic's hell, but not the end,
Stay in contact with your friend.

Stand away, two metres apart,
Social distancing, just the start.
Masks out handy, make-believe,
Clean this air for all to breath.

Paddy 26.03.20

"I wrote this during the 'Lock-Down'.
I was with my sister for the duration, as my partner is a class 1 driver for
Gregory's (for now) and due to my health problems I wasn't living with
him, it's been a very difficult time, but I always try to find some humour."

These Lockdown Blues

So after five weeks I am feeling quite bitter
Becoming a food laden lazy couch sitter
My Blitz spirit's nil and I need to get fitter
Oh these lockdown blues

Repeats on the TV, avoiding the news
It's far too depressing, 'Oh where are my shoes'?
They're fast growing cobwebs discarded in two's
Oh these lockdown blues

Awaiting the next vacant grocery slot
If I get one, elation!! Then followed by what
on earth can I get , what on earth have I got?
Oh these lockdown blues

Oh how I long for a seaside meander
A browse round the shops , I will now say with candour
that when I stand sideways I look like a panda
Oh these lockdown blues

So wearing pyjamas is my daily clothing
I'm filled up with grub and full of self loathing
I'm shutting up now as I'm sick of my moaning!!
Oh these lockdown blues!!

Jude West (Plymouth)

"I am Plymouth born and bred, but became a South African - Johannesburg is my home.

The South African government has a unique, some might call it bizarre, view of how we should be locked down, here. Purchasing alcohol and cigarettes was banned, for example. The alcohol ban was lifted a couple of days ago. Tobacco products remain banned, but no one knows why. There is a conspiracy theory that says a government minister is heavily involved in the black market.

As she is the ex-wife of ex-president Zuma, it is a strong possibility!

Can buy clothing, but not t-shirts or slops, or open-toed shoes!

Can only exercise for an hour or two, alone, during the morning (this ruling also relaxed a couple of days ago).

Strange times, indeed!"

Alan Osborne (Plymouth/Johannesburg, South Africa)

"I have lost my Mum in lockdown, had her funeral which was odd ,tried to support a daughter-in-law through cancer treatment and radiotherapy through this.
Have had to stay off work due to being bereaved and I am a nurse so have felt guilty about my colleagues struggling; it's been the worst time of my life ever.
I have been keeping a diary or log, here is just one entry for you to see."
Marion Roch (Plymouth)

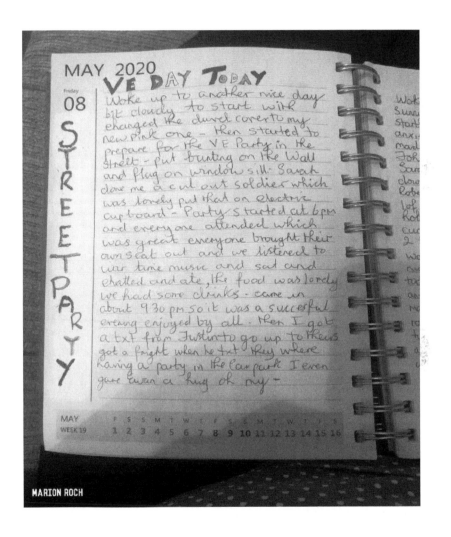

Music Lovers had to turn to HMV online or Amazon
whilst HMV remained closed

"All I can contribute is we have eaten and drank like we're on all inclusive holiday in our back garden.
I'm a shielder so staying in.
The only contact I have is with the fridge I'm afraid."
Leigh Armstrong (Plymouth)

"I guess the most enduring thing to me would be getting to know my neighbours, those living in my area, and local suppliers, feeling gratitude for their selflessness.
Localised websites that have been a lifeline and names of people living around me and getting to know them thru what they post on there. Gratitude for living amongst such a lovely community.
And on a more personal note, baking, cooking, sharing what we have, helping people to get what they need."
Anna Haffenden (Plymouth)

"I lost my gorgeous 99-year-old Grandad mid March (not Covid related) and Lock-Down came as we were sorting a lovely send off for him. Unfortunately, due to the restrictions placed upon us our beautiful goodbye to the man we were so proud of (Dunkirk veteran) became a tiny, socially distanced gathering that, although special, just didn't seem enough."
Julie Eaton (Plymouth)

The Early Days of Lockdown
25th March 2020

"Great idea for a book - a period that all of us will remember - some for exquisitely sad reasons.

I'm a full time artist, so am very fortunate in that nothing much changed. In fact, I found lockdown in it's most extreme phase quite liberating - no need to think about what I was going to wear for my hour of exercise daily because nobody would see me anyway, and that hour was spent with my husband and son (who otherwise would be at his girlfriend's or out with mates), enjoying and noticing with new eyes everything that had always been in front of us but had not been appreciated.

My son is an absolute Lego nerd, making animations, building, filming
(he's 17), so has enjoyed quality time with his passion.

I've attached a portrait that I did of him to capture him in this moment- it wasn't intended to be a Marvel advert - but comes across as such, but it puts this period in a nutshell for me.

*It's called '***Spending Time With Lego In Lockdown***'.*

Jo Beer (Plymouth)

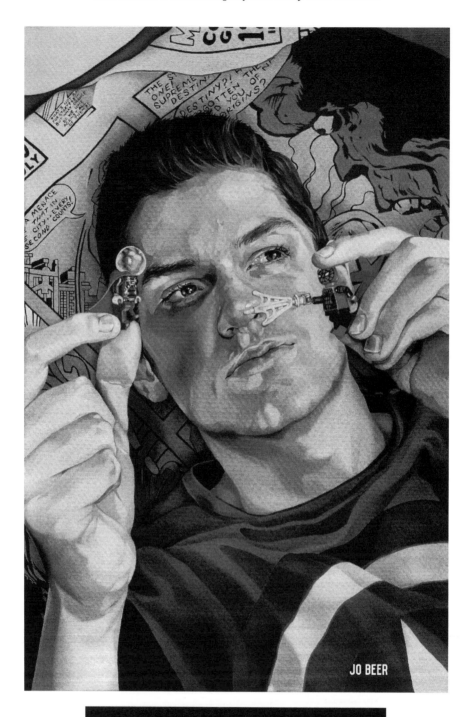

Spending Time With Lego in Lockdown

The 4 Walls of the Apocalypse

Hammer down this curtain call, the rise of evil, all man to fall,
These four walls, for health or hindrance, a barricade to our existence,
Mortal man, in worlds survive, behind closed doors, to stay alive,
But spare a thought for unseen illness, locked in head, we ask forgiveness.
This brutal enemy outside and in, is locked inside the walls of skin.

Sometimes up, most times low, this battle hard, try not to show,
No compromise to all who tell, were locked inside this prison cell.
To bang the head against the wall, we shout out loud, our voiceless call,
Hang on tight for the roads ahead, ring through this place, and all that's said.
These trying times, are hard on all, this mind of mind, try not to fall,
Into the darkness between this plight, staying strong, we all must fight.

We care, we share, we live and we laugh, with love we hold the pen to the graph,
Inside this mind, the battle rages, through cancerous thoughts, no one to save us.
Within these walls, my personal crypt, these four walls, the minds in bits,
Rest assured the curtain it calls, to the virus command, as men we fall.
Time will be the key.

Paddy

"It's been a difficult time for all, I think the hardest part of all this for myself was not being able to visit my family and vice versa, I've not given my mum or dad a hug since this all began - I work as a care assistant and my mum has COPD so I am unable to visit my parents at this time.

It's been hard for everyone not being able to visit families, meet up for lunch, going to the cinema, gym, work, park etc etc the list goes on. Hopefully, maybe, once this is over and eventually life gets back to some kind of normality and at present that's a big if with what is going on in the world at the moment such as the BLM, riots etc.

Hopefully one day people will wake up and be more civil and caring towards each other regardless of skin colour, sexual orientation, disabilities etc.

We have all been in this together, look around people and stop to think - yes life can be hard especially times like this but we can get through this we just all need to work together, stay safe and take care."

Deborah Hearson (Plymouth)

"It's been a crazy, scary time for all but somehow we seem to have managed; the hardest thing is that we can't see family and friends the way we would have liked, but we have survived."

Nikki Fellows (Plymouth)

"I would rather forget it."

John Harrison (Plymouth)

The Lockdown

Please stay in your home
If you do not have a home
You must self isolate
For at least 14 days
Remain in your room and
Maintain a safe distance

The news from abroad is not good
We are expecting numbers
To increase
Please wash your hands
For at least 20 seconds
Please stay in your home

There is no need to empty the shelves
Some people are stockpiling food
There is no need to visit your Mother
She will understand
Some people are gathering in numbers
There is no need for non essential journeys
But numbers have increased overnight

A range of items are still available
Keep a few essentials in your kitchen
Kitchen essentials can be very versatile
The kitchen is the heart of every home
And home is where the heart is
Please stay in your home
Until further notice

The Lockdown has been extended

But there is no need for alarm
You must follow these simple guidelines
And remain calm

It is important that we remain resolute
It is important we simply remain calm
Your Government remains resolute
Your leader is in good spirits
But remains unavailable at this time

It is essential that we focus
On the task in hand
It is essential that we remain
Single minded in our purpose
And give our total support
To Government agencies

Time is at the heart of the problem
And only time will tell
But until then
Until the numbers are no longer gathering
And I gather the numbers from abroad
Are not looking good
We must all remain in our homes
Find a safe room in the heart of your home
And stay there
We will keep you updated
There are a number of simple guidelines
You must follow

Journeys are no longer necessary
For maintaining a safe distance
By increasing hand washing time to 30 seconds
We can show our support
To essential Government agencies
It is essential that in our hearts
We do not stockpile increasing alarm
Your Mother will understand
Empty shelves can be very versatile

And we can expect Government guidelines to increase
But until then
Until we have the numbers
We have in our hearts
A home
And in that home
There is a room
And in that room
There is a shelf
And on that shelf
There is
Your Hope

Ed Tapper April 2020 (Plymouth)

"Roses are red, I was blue.
Lockdown is over.
How do you do?"
A Robert Farr (Plymouth)

*"My life has not changed.
Get up go work. Come home play computer games."*
Graeme Barber (Plymouth)

'Shit on it, Shit on it'…

The date was Friday 27th March 2020, the schools had kicked out and Lockdown had officially begun for The Hillary's and so did my 8 years olds obsession with Friday Night Dinner!

Now I'm pretty sure that when we were given a day off school for teacher training or a burst pipe we'd bound out of school, ties wrapped around our heads sprinting for the nearest park instead I was greeted with a playground full of kids and teachers crying… not my son, his first words were…

"Friday Night Dinner here we come."

Morning, noon and night (in between home schooling of course!!!) The familiar theme tune has been ringing in my ears. The dulcet tones of Jackie screaming at Martin echoing around my house. The pranks 'Puss Face' and 'Piss Face' play being re-in-acted at our dinner table. My son impersonating Jim and Wilson with fake dogs and glasses every time the bloody door goes. He is actually now starting to sound very Jim like on normal basis "hello mummy you look nice" has been perfected.

And then there's the on line zoom quizzes on a regular basis. For an 8 year old its pretty impressive that the quiz master asks -

"What name did Wilson's birthday balloon say" and immediately my kid answers "Lydia!" Out of 82 questions he got 4 wrong. If only he were that good at REN reading at school!

So there we have it, 4 months in, I've watched EVERY SINGLE EPISODE of this crap at least 5 times an episode and finally "shit on it, Shit on it" has now taken on a whole new meaning!

This leads nicely onto the other loves of his life… Fortnight, COD and Tik Toking!

Now as a 40 year old mummy who is completely out of touch with anything that requires technology I have found the whole business slightly confusing and frustrating to say the least. Confusing because I quite simply can not get my head around the excitement a 'virtual skin' provides or the entertainment that is known as 'Travis Scott' participating as a giant cartoon in a game of Fortnight whilst singing (if that's what you call it) about the weather, making it to the top and nose bleeds.

Frustrating because when I'm asked by my son to create a Tik Tok account I haven't a clue what it is or how to do it! I figure it out and before you know it I'm being drawn into supporting with the production of his videos (are they even called videos I ask myself!!) and being talked into buying and making props for such productions!

I mean 'Fortnight'… surely there is someone I can lodge a formal complaint with because this game has been ongoing for nearly 4 months not a bloody Fortnight, there really is no end in sight for this struggling

Mummy of one child!   I'm pretty sure 'Friday Night Dinner's' Martin would have a thing or two to say about the Internet and three of those words would be 'SHIT ON IT'!!!

All jokes aside, one thing I have been eternally grateful for is being able to spend an unprecedented amount time with my son and husband.

It's weird, we give birth to them, wean them, nurture them and guide them, then before you know it off to school they go and the teachers spend more time with our children than we do.

I have looked at this lockdown as a blessing rather than an inconvenience. It's enabled us as a family to reassess our lives and taught us to cherish and appreciate the simple things."

Laura Hillary (Plymouth)

The Early Days of Lockdown

Unlike now, the early days of 'Lockdown' were like something out of a nightmare. Remember the opening scenes in '28 Days Later'? That's just what it was like. The streets were fairly empty, with the pigeons and seagulls searching the areas for scraps to eat; difficult with no takeaways, pasty's or fast food scraps available.

The entrance to Drake Circus was very quiet…

The City Centre in March 2020

The seagulls have flown away…

The suns dips over New George Street

Blue Skies, bare trees, empty streets…

No 'action' outside Charles Cross Police Station

The wind whistles
Down the empty
Streets. passing
Empty buildings
In silence...

As the lights begin to dim, the streets are barely alive…

New George Street was now New 'Ghost Town' Street

Read the Signs

Remnants of the 'Black Lives Matter' Plymouth protest march.

The Great Toilet Roll Panic of 2020

After the Barbican 'chaos' during 'Lockdown', new signs appeared

All the planning, organising and preparing for a year of events that ended up being 'cancelled'…

As Quiet as a Church Mouse

With all of the Churches and places of praise not opening to the public during lockdown, behind closed doors the large and empty buildings were more quiet and peaceful than ever; but do we really need a large ornately decorated building to still have faith and you've gotta have faith, faith, faith...

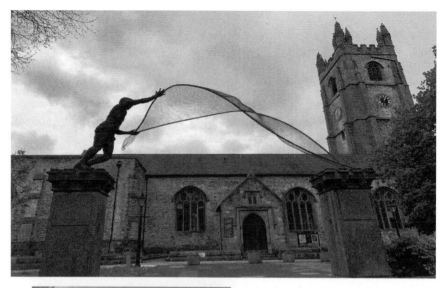

Lunchtime never seemed this quiet, it's oh so quiet…

*The Windows of the Church looked out into the world
and no one looked back in…*

Places were crying out to have people visiting once more…

The monument to Michael Foot in Freedom Fields Park –
Labour leader, lifelong Plymouth Argyle FC Supporter and son
of Plymouth.

The Sundial in the City Centre

An upturned table in Freedom Fields Park

"Like nothing we have ever encountered before…"

The buses were more empty than full, just taking keyworkers to work and returning them home again at the end of the day.

The sun goes down over New George Street

The view from the upper deck was always amazing

Early in the Lockdown, in the City Centre

Looking towards Royal Parade

Royal Parade at 6:18pm on 1st April

No Police, no robberies or break-ins – everyone was at home

Ebrington Street stands empty, no traffic, no people. Usually a thriving bar & café culture occurs, but not during the months of 'Lock-Down'. Only Sainsbury's and Tesco were open and thriving.

Buses were moved to a 'Sunday Service' everyday, which although was good for the drivers, it didn't help the keyworkers trying to get to and from work.

Where the streets had no cars...

NIGEL TAYLOR

The weather was there, the people weren't...

Wayward Life

Fragranced beauty lay in the air, a touch of fantasy, to all who care.
Lays golden sunlight on days of new, a brighter future comes in to view.
Winters warmth, wave's goodbye, as spring is searching, to comply,
The leaves are green, the flowers bloom, walk hand in hand, so very soon.

Birdsong musicals, clouds blue from grey, windswept trees, dance through the day.
Yellow daffodils, their scent so sweet, walking barefoot upon the beach.
Cascading waves, white horses break, sunlit golden, is ours to take.
Fresh gentle breeze, on wayward smiles, as bumblebees, in pollen lies.
True beauty in nature, as life slows down, enhanced by knowledge of life profound.

Paddy 31.03.20

"Just worn out from working and home schooling!!"
Kerry Warren (Plymouth)

"Lockdown for me has been a total change in my life.

It's been amazing in some ways, as we've never had so much time as a family. No children will be able to say they got to spend this much time at home (why didn't this happen when I was a kid?).

We've grown an allotment worth of veg plants, my youngest has learnt to ride his bike without stabilisers, I've not had to worry about work for months, no buses, no buses with the children!!

It's been amazing in so many ways!! But also so isolating.

I've had days where I've been miserable, maybe even depressed. It's been isolating and nerve wracking as someone with a medical condition that puts me in the vulnerable group.

I've been paranoid and panicked.

I've missed my friends and family, trying to explain to my kids why they can't see them has been the toughest, crying children makes any situation so much worse!

So I'll be glad when it's all over, I may even be happy to go to work again one day!!

Thank god for modern phones!"

Naomi Partridge (Plymouth)

"No friends and no family, was only surrounded by my own loneliness my mind built with thoughts and wonders of what will happen and plans began building.
Having more time to think about myself and my future rather than living in the present, I had to adapt to believe and live in the future and what it withholds."

Jazmine Gilbert (Plymouth)

A Description of Covid-19 By Oliver Tanner Age 11

I was born in China I grew out of control,
Spreading across countries making people look so bold
Moving city to city town to town, infecting the sick and elderly making the
continents go in lockdown.

Soon people were perishing unable to stop me raging across Europe
panic buying making stocks go dry,
World leaders collide in heating debate trying to stop me the best they
came up with self-isolation for weeks.
Medicine is in development trying to find a cure a barrier to stop me from
getting anywhere "to turn the tide",
Humans trying so hard to stop me ruining the world economy's crashing
making prices sky high,
Shops closing down speeches making everyone frown in twelve weeks we
will have the cure, the NHS they seem so sure,
Working tirelessly around the clock, putting themselves at risk of my very
own iron fist."
Oliver Tanner (Plymouth)

"*I should qualify my entry by stating that although I work in Plymouth I do not live there these days but I had done for many years before crossing the water where me and my other half (The Beardy One) rent a place in a small seaside village just over the water in Cornwall.*

Pre-Covid, having often bemoaned the time I spend travelling to and from work I wondered if the whole working from home situation I have found myself in since March would be a case of 'be careful what you wish for'.

In short... no!

Although I have missed bouncing ideas off colleagues and the general buzz around the office, having more time at home (and saving a fortune in fuel) has been fantastic!

The Beardy One is set up in the kitchen but my 'office' is in a dilapidated van overlooking the sea. My company is the sound of the sea and the various birds singing away - it is glorious!

Either side of our place - in a row of 6 ex-coastguard cottages - are second homes. Only two of the cottages in the row are actually lived in. The cottages either side of us are second homes - one side owned by a lovely couple from London whose family hail from the area, the other side an older couple from Gloucestershire who have nothing good to say about anything or anyone! We've missed seeing one lot... the others not so much!

My family are all hundreds of miles away so I have missed visiting them, but having video calls has been brilliant. Reminds me of scenes from programmes like The Waltons (ask Alexa, kids!) when whole families gathered round their radios, only now it's a phone or tablet and it talks back!!!!

A (dis)honourable mention should go to the members of the 'Heart of the South West' pirate crew for making the best of a bad lot by staying in touch and setting daft challenges to keep us all amused.

And a shout out to the many bands and artists playing lockdown sets to keep themselves and us on the right side of sanity. Shout outs to Felix of The Captain's Beard, Miles Hunt and in particular JollyRoger for being instrumental in hosting many virtual festivals in these gig-free months. You have done wonders!

All in all I have had a positive experience of lockdown - mainly due to living with someone who is as daft as me, but also in part because I have done my best to avoid the scaremongering on social media!

The situation has been helped hugely by working for an employer who I have to say has gone the extra mile to make this all do-able without shedding jobs. For that I salute them. I wish you all the best - and as this eases, remember... Don't be a knob!

Kirsty Tonks (Portwrinkle, Cornwall)

The lack of people was evident on dog walks...

LEMMINGS

POOR OLD HOE
HERE THEY COME
CHARGE OF THE LEMMINGS
HAS BEGUN

IN SMELLY CARS
ON NOISY BIKES
EVERYONE DOING
WHAT HE LIKES

WHERE ARE THEY FROM
WHERE DO THEY GO
WHY DO THEY HAVE TO
CIRCLE THE HOE

WHAT ARE THEY AFTER
WHAT DO THEY NEED
WHEN THEY GET ROUND
WHAT IS ACHIEVED

IS IT A PENANCE
IS IT A DARE
EVER STOP TO LOOK
AT WHAT IS THERE

FANTASTIC VIEW
GLORIOUS SEA
WHY BUGGER IT UP
FOR YOU AND ME

MET, JUNE 2020

"Having been furloughed from work, and away from my home and family in Australia, I have taken time to notice all the good that has been occurring.

From neighbours reconnecting and looking out for each other, kind gestures from the community and the constant contact from friends and colleagues.

I put a lot of this positive energy into reconnecting with arts and crafts, baking, jogging, reading and just enjoying the chance to slow down.

I took courses for work and learnt new skills.

It was a great chance to re-gather and reconnect.

A tough time indeed but I took the chance to make the most of it."

Loz E. Hogan (Plymouth)

"I am disabled and housebound.

So to me - and many like me - lockdown is a routine. That's no to say it did not impact me.

My daughter Nicole - my live in carer - initially struggled with the shopping. People panic buying caused shortages of essentials. There were toilet roll jokes galore on Facebook.

The effort and bravery of hospital staff was humanity at its best.

The loss of life to those on the front line regardless of colour was heart-breaking as was all the loss of loved ones and sorry to say it's not over yet.

I have expressed my opinion re Boris and cronies efforts elsewhere. I hope and pray he remembers to give nurses a pay rise reflecting there true worth to the people..."

Richard Brock (Plymouth)

"My memory is of sadness.
I sadly lost my 99yr old mum to this awful virus, she was so looking forward to her party we were planning. A cremation with only 10 people allowed in Guildford so an early morning start from Tavistock a 20 min service a short visit to her home and a drive all the way back home, no hugs with my brothers. Doesn't feel like I've said goodbye.
Because of the restrictions regarding funerals my family; I have many cousins etc, felt they wanted to do a tribute to my mum who knitted many many personalised Christmas stockings, so they made bunting from photographs and did a guard of honour for her on her final journey through her home town."

Janette Lown (Tavistock)

"Our 'lockdown cul de sac' social distancing days."
Abby Vanstone (Plymouth)

"So I was furloughed the last Thursday in March. Since then I have completely redecorated my house and transformed our garden into a utopic state.

I have a real passion for '80s music and in between the chore that lay ahead I - along with my very good friend and RUSH nut Adrian Grainger - recorded 12 classic '80s songs in my recording studio. These can be found on Facebook.

Also having bags of time as I throw myself in DIY mode I've been playing all my vinyl albums, which I totally love.

It's been very weird to say the least, I still am unsure what the future holds and quite frankly it does scare me to a degree. So I'll carry on recording and taking my Schnauzer Reg out for his 3 walks and enjoy what life is really all about.

Love caring and nature.

I have 3 sons and a daughter Alex 30...Yes he is named after Mr Lifeson xx Sam 29, Dominic 26 and Libby 22. Needless to say they now also have immaculate houses... THANKS DAD!!!"

Simon Young (Plymouth)

"My thoughts on lockdown and how it changed our lives.

There were so many positives from lock down. That one-hour exercise per day gave my wife and I the opportunity to really explore the immediate area we live in and we discovered so much more about where we live, Keyham. We enjoyed walking and found places that were fantastic and just on our doorstep.

We even discovered a Woodpecker family at Pounds Park so went most nights to check on them.

As lock down eased we went further afield and revisited places we'd forgotten about.

So all in all it's had a positive effect on us. So I decided to sum it up in some poetry:

Quiet roads, clear skies, it's eerie.
Where have all the contrails gone?

Birds singing, they're happy. Ignorant of our world and what's going on.
Days at home with the family on 80%, it's priceless; I'll happily take that cut in pay.
Miss the pub, I'm drinking too much, I'm sure I'll cut down at the end of May.

Walks with the wife, most evenings when quiet.
Not too far, you've only got an hour.
"I'll make some scones tomorrow" she says, if only I could get some bloody flour!

The lockdown is eased, we are so pleased, we walk - not taking the double decker.
It's Pounds Park tonight, what a wonderful sight it's home to the great spotted Woodpecker!

Night after night we walk with delight to see if the young chicks have grown.
What a wonderful place, it's stunning, so nice and we'd forgotten, we say with a groan.

There's more, Radford, Warleigh, Lopwell and Plym we're so lucky, it's like we're in Heaven!
It's not an apple but a walk that keeps the Doc away, especially when you're in this part of Devon!

It's the birdsong for me that I'll remember with glee, the Song Thrush and Blackbird in trees such as Acers.
Singing so sweetly but not loud enough to silence those bloody boy racers!"

Mike Carey (Plymouth)

Even in the middle of the day it was very
quiet, very empty, very lonely…

'Warning Signs' appeared quickly all over Plymouth as shops, libraries, museums and offices tried to warn off the thieves and would be chancers, who might've thought that the empty properties might have been easy pickings...

Royal Parade, lunchtime

"Never in all my days did I ever think that I would live through a global pandemic; life became very surreal, and uncertain.
For me - as I suspect for a lot of people - it gave myself the opportunity to reset, take stock, and move forward."
Paddy Mullen (Plymouth)

Lock-Down: A Time for Recollection

"So lockdown has been a bit mental.

Whilst I recognise that it's been entirely necessary, it hasn't half been a boring time. Filled largely with sitting at home doing nothing, it has been a real slog at times trying to manufacture the motivation to get up and be productive.

However, thanks to the huge increase in free time, it has allowed me to dabble in a new hobby, film photography.

I've been interested in photography for many years now, and particularly have always loved the look of 35mm photography but have always felt like I haven't had the time or the means to give it a go.

Well, that changed during lockdown, I bought myself a 35mm camera, some film, did my research, research, research and endeavoured to get out and shoot my surroundings, and I've been incredibly pleased with the results so far!

For reference, I've never had any formal training or education in photography, and all I've learned is purely through my research online, but please enjoy this sample of some of my favourite shots I've taken so far, and if you've like to see any more going forward you can find me on Instagram at josh.macaulay or on Flickr as jlmshots35.

Peace out."

Josh Macaulay (Plymouth)

JOSH MACAULAY

"What has lockdown in Plymouth meant for me?
The first few days of walking through the empty city centre was pretty eerie like something out of the movies, but it quickly became the norm not to see anybody.
After the initial panic of working out how to juggle work and instantly becoming a teacher to ensure schoolwork was completed we quickly fell in to a routine with the only problem being each day was very similar to the one before.
Eat, sleep, work, repeat!
Did I miss going out for a drink? Not really.
Did I miss being able grab a coffee on the way to work? Not really.
Did I miss sport on the tele? Not really.
Did I miss just being able to pop to the shop and pick up something random? A little bit.
Did I miss popping in to see family and friends? Absolutely."
David Hyatt (Plymouth)

Everyone tried to get through the 'Lock-Down' with a little humour and light relief, even the local cemeteries got in on the action, trying to ease people's minds and worry families less than they needed to.

"Lockdown for me as a carer for my disabled son is we have been in for 15 weeks, not seeing anyone other than neighbours over the fence, family via phone calls and a few trusted friends who helped getting shopping and prescriptions.

It became lonely at times missing that adult conversation.

Mother's day not seeing my mum or myself seeing my daughter, grandchildren and son was hard when you could tell more cars were on the road.

A friend Gill whom we meet through going to see PAFC would call every Tuesday at 3pm outside the fence socially distanced to have a chat. This meant so much to us both.

The 1st 'Clap for Carers' was surreal as it was still dark at 8pm.

The most silly moment was when doing the dishes I said to my son "this is my PPE, my rubber gloves". I put it up on Facebook as it made us laugh to be followed by friends posting photos of their rubber gloves. For a few hours it gave us a giggle and others wondering why are you taking photos of rubber gloves.

Still can't believe what we have gone through and will the norm will it ever be the same again?"

Susan Clark and Family (Plymouth)

Lockdown for me has felt very surreal almost like a ghost town.

Very few cars on the roads, people in the street.

However, I have felt an enormous coming together of my community. All helping each other, helping the vulnerable and looking out for each other more.

Home-schooling has been very tough, and I feel so much for my daughter who is struggling to comprehend, why she can't hug or see her friends and family outside our family unit.

Lockdown has been very weird, and very challenging, but it's brought us all closer together."

Anne Martin (Plymouth)

"Walking down the middle of silent, car free streets.

Strangers saying hello, smiling or a nod to acknowledge the strangeness.

The quiet - hearing a train depart Plymouth station from 1 mile away on the Hoe."

Hilary Phillips Kolinsky (Plymouth)

"Shielding from 17th March. Many desperate dark days feeling very anxious and worried. Feeling very isolated and lonely. Lots of tears. Looking through a window at my new grandson, totally heartbreaking."

Brenda Mullan (Saltash)

"The one thing that struck me was the quiet.
I live in Torpoint, across the river from the dockyard and one evening, a few days after the lockdown had started, I went into the front garden and looked out over the river towards the main yard complex. For the first time I could ever remember there was no thumping and grating of heavy machinery drifting across but this allowed sounds I had never noticed before to become apparent.
The city itself had stopped and I could hear the world as it was meant to be before we came along and put our stamp onto everything.
For a moment it felt as if there was nobody else around and I was the only human left.
Strange and dystopian times."
Mary Hallett (Torpoint)

"Lockdown 2020, alone, secluded, listening to the news, watching the death toll.

My mental wellbeing decreasing and unable to get to my 'patch', Dartmoor. It's the one place that helps me relax, exercise, lift my spirits. Social distancing would be impossible in my local park, and it holds bad memories for me.

I left my job to become self-employed at the end of 2019. New year, new start, living the dream!!

A couple of months of getting prepared and then find a part time job to keep my bills paid until I got established...

Suddenly there were no jobs available in my field, people furloughed, fears of redundancies. The self-employed got pay outs based on their last three years and I had nothing. I applied for key worker vacancies, but without success. My CV is too office professional, not customer service based for a supermarket, yet I think I would have enjoyed it.

It reached the stage where I had to apply for Universal credit, then having to wait a further 5 weeks with knowing it doesn't actually cover my bills, let alone allow me to pay for food. My search continues and I'm applying for virtually anything and everything with a looming quarterly electricity bill, my bank account almost depleted.

It seems like almost everyone is applying at the moment.

Four weeks down the line and I still haven't heard anything back about my application for reducing council tax, yet they expect you to still pay until you get an outcome. Well, I no longer can.

Initially, I joined in with all the memes regarding toilet rolls; it did strike me as funny at the time. The novelty soon wore off, as the scaremongering left the shelves empty and I started to get concerns over pet food. I admit I placed more of that in my trolley than I normally would. I could go without myself, but not my animals.

It took me four weeks to brave a food shop after the lockdown was put in place. I was anxious about what I would have to do. The queuing, one-way systems, glass barriers. Turned out that it wasn't so bad in reality. I built it up to be much more than it was.

What I couldn't do was get the food I'd normally head for. Eggs, self-raising flour, bread flour and yeast being the main ones. I turned to Facebook for egg supplies, they were brilliant, and I ended up digging out an old bag of flour from the back of the cupboard and sifting out a couple of spiders. It was only for personal use, but I've since managed to get a fresh bag in, thankfully!

Instead of setting myself up, I took time out to sew scrub hats and drawstring bags for the NHS. I felt that I needed to do something constructive that would help in some way. It was a good excuse to finally try and use my overlocker and it was a struggle to work out how to even thread it! I got there, it no longer worries me and I learnt something that will prove very useful to me. All in all, it was a good experience.

Happy Birthday to me! That day arrived. I couldn't see anyone, I couldn't go anywhere. Sat on my own, yet really, I wasn't. A friend left me a card and a bunch of flowers on my doorstep; I had phone calls, text messages, Facebook messages. It virtually took up the whole day with all the chatting! It was a welcomed distraction.

Finally I got back to Dartmoor.

The sheep were just as interested in seeing me, as I was them! They almost came over to me. The ponies, they actually did. I got to scratch the tops of their heads as they snuffled and gummed me. It was an incredible feeling to be back! I used to climb tors like a goat, but I've lost my flexibility and strength by staying indoors. I need to build myself back up again.

There were several tents, although no overnight stays allowed, the left over barbecues. Not so much in camper vans, but they were parked around Burrator in 'inconspicuous' white Combo vans. I couldn't say where they came from, whether local or not. Apart from the barbecues, the actual camping didn't affect me so much.

Still very socially distanced, unlike the packed beaches and the protests. It's not just me that needs a mental health boost, so I understand why. I didn't witness the littering, but fires are definitely a concern.

We're at the stage where it is the first weekend that people can travel and through an RAC poll, it was estimated that 630,000 plan to go camping. I sincerely hope they don't all aim for here, and for those who do, that they look after the environment. Most of all, leave some room for me!! I've had events postponed; ironically including Ranulph Fiennes 'Living Dangerously' tour at the Pavilions.

Music bands have rescheduled, but it's looking like the new dates won't be possible either. The uncertainty must be so frustrating for them, but I've enjoyed the live streaming – The Alarm have had big night ins for sixteen Saturday evenings, IAMX have had live performances on Crowdcast, I'm watching the second 'Let's Rock Lockdown' Fest this evening, I've enjoyed Gok Wan DJ'ing from his kitchen with his 'Isolation Nation', which he now intends to make a reality.

Finally, I joined in with over 100,000 people worldwide, watching the sunset over Stonehenge for the summer solstice, courtesy of the English Heritage.

Well done these people! Will there be a second wave? I don't know. It doesn't look favourable. What I do know is that I will continue to remain careful for as long as it takes to be safe again."

Di Newman (Plymouth)

The beautifully stunning cloudless blue skies meant that although the parks were mostly empty still, the beaches were over subscribed and at the point of causing a second wave and a tighter more strict 2nd Lockdown…

"I think that lockdown has been great in reminding people to slow down and appreciate the little things in life. In many ways it's what people needed whether they knew it or not, as it has taught people to slow down and take time for yourself and family and that you don't have to fill every waking hour with random stuff you do even though you find it a chore.

It certainly made me and I'm pretty sure most of the population how important family is and to cherish every moment you spend with them no matter how annoying they can be.

Covid 19 has made me think about how we need to slow down mass consumerism and the throw away society we have created in order to give the planet a fighting chance of recovery from all the crap we have done to it.

Most of all the lockdown has made me realise I have amazing willpower as I didn't give in and bury the kids under the patio."

Simon Jones (Plymouth)

"Lock down has been a long time without seeing friends, and a big worry looking after the elderly."
Jackie Duncan (Saltash)

"What the lockdown has meant for me; we know it's been an emotional rollercoaster, from total isolation for weeks on end, not being able to see family or friends, never knowing if a cough or high temperature would be the death of you and your loved ones.

Constantly worrying because you live alone would you die alone? And if you did, who would know?

Worrying whether or not you could get your medications on time always being on edge, listening to the news every day hearing how many people worldwide had died with this virus.

But on the other side of things - having great family and friends to help keep you going. Helping with shopping, getting your medications for you helping to keep you sane with 'Facetiming' and just staying in touch with everyone.

I am so grateful for having such great family and friends I've missed you all and can't wait for this to all be over so we can all be together again."
Marilyn Jones (Plymouth)

"It has been very strange in Plymouth.
Not seeing out the football season yet still gaining promotion. Hunting for toilet rolls!!! Always having my key worker letter at hand should I be asked why l was travelling. Not seeing relatives, missing birthday do's and no meals in restaurants or visits to the pub.
Seeing the brand new leisure centre (Barcode) closed."
Paul Paskins (Ipplepen)

"I suffer with ischemic heart failure so didn't go out very much apart from hospital and doctors appointments.

Taking my dogs out if they didn't have a walker and on a Saturday my neighbour would take me shopping at Tesco so to be honest I didn't notice much difference when lockdown first started.

Then it seemed a bit strange when my friends who would usually visit twice a week and also take my dogs out for me weren't coming.

My neighbour still brought me a roast every Sunday but would leave it on my patio table for me to collect, so I wasn't having any human contact, I still didn't think it bothered me until when I saw other dog walkers while walking mine I realised rather than a quick hello I was keeping them talking for a good half hour.

After about three weeks of lockdown my friends husband started coming to take the dogs out, I would put their leads on my garden table and he would collect them from there, it felt pretty safe because I wasn't in contact with anyone else and neither was he apart from his wife I was 99% sure neither of us had it.

When they introduced the bubble they both became mine.

Two weeks ago I asked my (bubble) friend if she would take me to draw some cash out as I had run out so she took me to Tesco post office, I must say all the morning while waiting for her to turn up I was feeling physically sick with nerves and when I finally got there I was shaking like a leaf and actually burst into tears, the cashier was lovely and was making sure I was ok. I explained that I found it such a daunting experience as that was the first time I had actually been anywhere since I started shielding and never experienced the 2mtr rule etc.

I have been out with the dogs but that was in a field right beside where I live but apart from that I hadn't been out. So that's pretty much my story."

Jan Wilson (Plymouth)

"For us it's been a chilled out time, it's given us all a chance to slow down our pace and it's been quite surreal considering how long Jamie and I have been together the initial lockdown we were both working from home, before I was made furloughed. Me, being furloughed, was his excuse to take a break to go for a walk something he has always been too exhausted or not had enough time to do. If you check out Jamie Parr photography you will see his camera started to come out with us.

For Jake as a 17yr old the school have been very concerned about mental wellness however, it's given him the boost to find a job so he became a key worker by working in Iceland and became one of the hundreds they recruited to be able to meet demand of home delivery."

Lisa Willis (Plymouth)

"My life in lockdown has been a bit difficult.
Not the greatest time to go through a break up and still be living
in the same house.
A rollercoaster of emotions.
Trying to be strong, considerate, kind.
Working through feelings of guilt and doubt.
Up and down. Up and down.
Not being able to 'pop out' to see a friend for a chat and talk
through things. On the other hand... it made me realise things I
take for granted every day and made me feel humbled.
It's given me clarity on some things and the opportunity to 'slow
down' (I was always rushing somewhere).
The simple things are the best."
Jennifer Docking (Plymouth)

Enigma

What dreams are these that line this mind, secrets inside for me to find,
Lay cast this shadow on all mankind, for I am but an enigma.
I open my eyes to the golden sun, and close the past, to things that I've done,
I pull the trigger to this smoking gun, for I am but an Enigma.

A message to you, is all that I say, pay homage to new, as you battle the day,
On the frontline, paving the way, for you are but an Enigma.
We light the fires, that burn this true path, silence our voice, to the biblical wraith,
Reset one another, take chances in half, for life is but an enigma.

Frontline commando's that work in the store, supplying the fuel for us to endure,
Securing the fort, so noble and pure, for they are all enigmas.
So youngest at heart, these houses we burn, lighting the flame, we each take a turn,
Longing forgiveness, this feeling I yearn, and the past was just an enigma.

Look to the future, as things all seem clear, holding you close, those that hold dear,
Riding the storm, embrace all you fear, for time is just an enigma.
Carry the burden, as life gets in way, the edge of tomorrow, at end of the day,
We humans as one, on here we shall stay, for we are all but enigmas.

Paddy 4.04.20

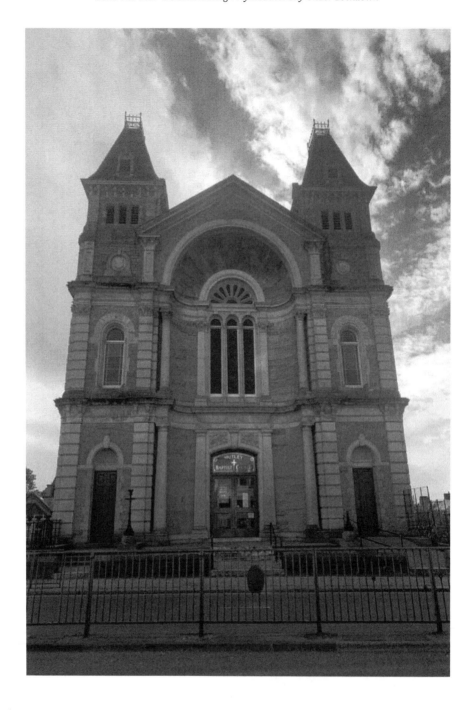

"So, lockdown for me has been strange.
Home for 8 weeks before I could work due to vulnerability.
I was in a state of shock at not getting up to go to work.
The first week felt like I was on holiday but it soon started to make me feel how alone and cut off I was.
I went out once a week for shopping and have kept to that routine throughout. The roads were quiet and places were hushed but I could hear birds and bees and not traffic.
I kept busy in the garden and read but I couldn't sleep. I'd still be awake at 4 in the morning. As time has gone on I'm now working but the sleep hasn't improved and I still hate being home with no social contact other than my husband.
However, I really have grown to hate the cars on the roads and inconsiderate people ignoring the rules. But I've loved how nature has carried on.
I've had a birthday and so many plans to celebrate that had to be cancelled like everyone else.
So, in conclusion to say it's been a strange time is an understatement and apart from my escape from the house to go grocery shopping I've had time to breathe and stop and reflect. And I don't want things to be like they were I've decided.
Things I've missed the most other than going to work for the social interaction?
Football.
And what a time to have lockdown when the season was at a crucial stage. Not going to see West Ham fighting to stay in the Premier or my local team Torquay trying to get into League 2.
But in the great scheme of things there have been other more important things to worry about. Unless you believe what the great Bill Shankly said and that there's nothing in the world more important that the great game."
Penny Southern (Newton Abbot)

"Everyone is helping everyone else let's hope it continues."
Paul Moss (Plymouth)

The sun was out; the parks were empty –
except for people doing their hour of daily exercise.

The Buses were mostly 'double-deckers' and usually empty, many travelling the desolate streets of Plymouth with only the driver on-board. Bus timetables were also altered and many buses worked on an hourly service.

Death by the Future

As the air around us weakens, and the ambiance of day dissolves,
Lay sleep among the shadows, as man and beast evolve.
Like zombies we mimic the dead, like rats in a race we can't win,
We close ourselves to the madness, and to all that could have been.

We listen for the sweet sound of silence, this time and place so alluring,
Locked deep in our own little kingdom, and ponder the event that's occurring.
Isolation, desperation, social depravity, as times in here all too hard,
The shops and streets all but empty, as this predator enter our yard.

People we think that ask questions, danger of death will suffice,
So before you go out on your jollies, listen to the government's advice.
No morals, no warning, no deadline, no script as were all blind to see,
No masts or big aerials rising, all in the name of 5G.

Throw heed to the error of caution, steel pillars that reach to the sky,
As cancerous waves all engulf us, hiding behind all the lie.
For now is the time to fight, say no to the future mankind,
Radiation to hide all our wrinkles, a new beginning for all man survived.

So put on your tinfoil helmets, and cover your face with a mask,
As viruses, bugs and integrity, deciding how long this will last.
Death from the future is closer, like numbers, we flash on the screen,
Lay waste to the error of mankind, and all that the future has seen.

Paddy 21.04.20

"This is a piece of art I completed fairly early in the lockdown when everyone was still clapping for the NHS workers.
I wondered how long this appreciation of their heroic deeds would actually last, and if things would change once Covid-19 is over.
The day I completed the piece I sold it for £200 and donated the money to the NHS Charities Together. Since then we've stopped clapping, and their is talk of all the brave student nurses who stepped in to the battlefield and risked their lives to save others, losing their contracts and not being offered permanent work, let alone a pay restructure to reflect their efforts.
All the political rhetoric of the moment seems to have been just that.
As lockdown eases we are distracted away from any political issues by footballers on the terraces, bodies on the beaches, and a return to the shopping malls.
But, as the saying goes, 'it's not over till the fat lady sings'."
Stephen James Beer (Saltash nr. Plymouth)

"I can honestly tell you as a concrete mixer driver who has pretty much worked through the lockdown that I have never poured so many bases for hot tubs! Plymouth back gardens must be getting full of them now."
Dave Perryman (Plymouth)

"I'm the guitarist for The Malthusian Trap.
Over the lockdown we released a song, made a music video using footage donated to us by fans from all around the world, wrote music together through the internet and made a weekly podcast talking about all things but Covid 19, as we wanted to take people's minds off our collective situation."
James Cox (Plymouth) www.malthusiantrap.co.uk

"*My name is Tina Price and I worked through it all in the finance industry.*

It was a difficult time for my colleagues as it was for everyone.

It seemed surreal coming into work when the streets were empty and not knowing what we would have to deal with when we came into the office. We also had a lot of staff that had to shield, so the workforce was scarce. It was scary, busy and unreal all at the same time.

It was also lonely going home and not being able to see my friends and family as I live by myself.

I have never used social media this much in all my life but it was the only way I could keep in touch with people.

I was also hoping to go on a coffee date with a gentleman, which didn't happen due to the lockdown so my dating life also went by the wayside.

I am glad we have made it through but this was a lonely and difficult time."

Tina Price (Plymouth)

"I've lived in this city all my life.
To walk through town on a Saturday afternoon with barely another soul in sight was so peaceful but eerie.
This lockdown made me really appreciate the important things in life. Not the materialistic but the ones I love and how I miss them."
Sarah Angela Regan (Plymouth)

"A photo of Poppy during lockdown, I think it's sad, as we love going to the park, but it's also funny, as she's trying to look cool!"
Bridgette Stanbury (Plymouth)

What it Means to Me

When I first heard about this virus
Sheer panic set in.
This was like something out of a horror movie.
The amount of people ill and dying was worrisome.
Not seeing your children or grandchildren just for a cuddle or a hug.
Everything you take for granted
Visiting your friends and family.
Having a coffee or lunch out was gone.
My son Sam sings in a band and we loved going to Annabel's and various pubs and venues, going to McDonalds 2am in the morning afterwards.
Trying to buy basic commodities, you couldn't get a slot for deliveries from supermarkets or had to wait for weeks. The mad panic for toilet roll and hand wash.
I remember the week before lockdown people filling trolleys with these items and I remember saying to my daughter Sarah, don't people wash their hands normally. Not realising they were looking ahead. My husband and I try to do one job a day to keep normality as much as possible exercise most days.
I also had dental problems so couldn't see the dentist for 3 months.
Acceptance soon comes and you abide by the rules
We distanced and had local deliveries.
It has made me appreciate everything so much more.
Our Church is closed so we have zoom internet it is not the same you do not have the feeling of togetherness the closeness of friends.
Shopping is easier now the items more readily available.
Now as lockdown is lifting we see family in the garden separate but together."

Shirley Rogers (Plymouth)

"What a fantastic idea, love this."
Karen Fleet (Plymouth)

"So I've been told to shield, this has been the hardest 8 and a half weeks of my life.
I never thought I would miss human interaction so much.
I did have a light that kept me going, my kids! I have a 12-year-old son and a 2-year-old daughter and if it wasn't for them, and my beautiful understanding wife I wouldn't have been able to get past this.
Lockdown for me gave me the opportunity to get to know my children, which I never thought possible. It also let me get to know myself.
I am a lot stronger than I thought I was."
Stuart Berry (Plymouth)

"One of the things I haven't liked about it is that some people haven't social distanced hence having no regard for anyone.
NHS have done an incredible job and those connected to it ie. ambulance drivers, teachers frontline workers etc. the list is endless .
I've loved how most have pulled together in this time.
The worse thing about it for me personally was not being able to hug and kiss my children and grandchildren."
Jennifer Hobbs (Plymouth)

"One of the things that has stuck out for me is this; do we really need all the material things we work so hard to buy?
I've got a 4 bedroom lovely house, two BMWs parked in our drive.
I work crazy hours and crazy shifts (as does my husband) and really why?
Do we need all of this?
The answer is no we don't! We need time together, we need peace of mind, we need our health, we need society, and we need friend's neighbors and family. We really don't need all of the 'stuff' the adverts on the Telly box so subliminally tell us we need.
Capitalism is not the way forward for me now at least.
We have never had the time to reflect before have we?
Now we can sit and work out what's really beneficial to enhancing our lives and it's not material things that's for sure.
However I'm sure once this is over most will return to the hamster wheel thinking they need the money."
Leigh Armstrong (Plymouth)

"Used my furlough as practice for retirement in 5 years.

Ate and drunk to much. Didn't go anywhere, was probably the weirdness thing.

The wife found me loads of DIY jobs which I've got done.

Hardest thing was cancelling our holiday in Southend to stay with our daughter and son-in-law. We don't see them often and missed out on that occasion.

Did also manage to do a lot of arty stuff which I love. Did this painting of Smeatons Tower.

Only downside I'm still furloughed so that's a worry.

(March 26th 2020. Photo I took at 5pm of Embankment Rd.)"

Ian Gus Hudson (Plymouth)

"I didn't find it much different as I am currently disabled and I taught myself how to paint over lockdown - that's it, I only learnt how to paint." **Lorraine Carroll (Plymouth)**

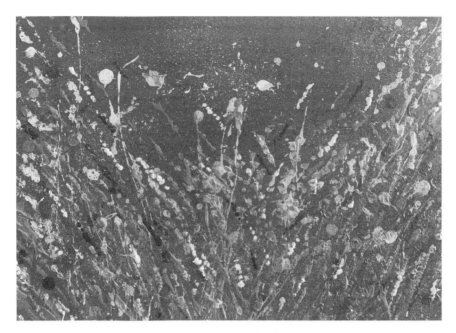

7 Day Survival

The first day we were told, to stay the hell inside,
But most of us ignored, and corona virus thrived.
Most ran to the shops, the stores were all in chaos,
As the country began to realise, that this virus is here to slay us.

Day two it saw the explosion, of face book courses for all,
And musicians and artist alike, adhered to hear the call.
The situation was getting serious; the numbers of dead were rising,
As the leaders of this country, their plans for us comprising.

Day three it saw the boredom, at least two meters wide,
As we all went about our business, and not indoors where we are
confined.
This country was on lockdown, the ignorant carried on,
For deaths around the corner, for them it won't be long.

Day four it saw the nation, rejoice for workers the key,
Be safe, be kind stay vigilant, so we can all be free.
We clapped, we cheered applauded, the medical staff online,
It all helps to fight this fight, and to slow the number of dying.

Day five we all sat watching, as Boris himself got sick,
To isolation now he's gone his own rules for him to stick.
Only leave the house, a brisk walk is all we can achieve,
But together as one we can do this, we all just have to believe.

Day six it fell on Saturday, we all managed to survive the days,
As mothers, daughters loved and loved ones fight back the boredom
craze.
The weather for once it lifted, the moods of family and friends,
Stuck indoors where we can ponder, when will all this shit end.

Day seven has finally reached us; the first week is all but finished,
There's light at the end of the tunnel, shop shelves are all but replenished.
Survival is all just a mind set; the streets lay bare in the towns,
The first week of all of this madness, right here in this lockdown.

Paddy 29.03.20

Pets During Lockdown

Pepper posing for Josh's Camera

Stanley out for a morning walk

The old Wooden Animals of New George Street

Just Stanley…

During the 'Lockdown' the people of Plymouth still did not lose their sense of humour or their 'community spirit'. People spent time talking to friends on internet services like Zoom, Skype and Houseparty, as well as making videos for their absent friends.

Post pandemic City Centre starter kit.

JUSTIN KELSO

Destination Nowhere

From the bedroom to the kitchen, from the toilet to the door,

Destination nowhere, as I repeat this day once more.

Put the kettle on, have a brew, nothing more for me to do.

Watching TV, washing hands, listening vigorously to government commands,

My destination's nowhere.

Missing loved ones call on phone, feeling desolate, not alone.

Staying positive, living life, double edged, just like a knife.

Writing poetry, reading book, one more chance to take a look.

Eating junk food, gaining weight, hair is long, need a break.

Getting through, each day by day, staying safe, it's the only way.

 Keeping dreams, to stay alive, take no chance, we must survive.

Love is sacred, all can tell, will get us through this living hell.

Loving girlfriend, miss so much, waiting for the gentle touch.

Go to bed, to dream once more, stay inside we all implore.

Saving fate, the futures bright, we all must stand to take this fight.

Switching channels face book stare, till once again we can breathe the air.

Ever hopefully, making plans, fidget finger on rubber bands,

This destination nowhere.
Paddy 26.03.20

Locked Up…

In the 'Lockdown'…

CURSE OF THE HOE

AS YOU STAND IN THE SUN
WATCHING FOLKS HAVE FUN
THE CURSE OF THE HOE
ROARS BY

IT'S A LAD AND A LASS
BOLD AS BRASS
AND THE CAR
HE'S TRYING TO FLY

IT'S SHINY AND CLEAN
LOOKS LOW AND MEAN
AND BOTTOMS
ON EVERY HUMP

IN A FUNNY WAY
YOU'RE FORCED TO SAY
THEY REMIND YOU
OF PRESIDENT TRUMP

BEING SOMEWHERE
THAT'S SWELL
AND MAKING IT
HELL

MET, MAY 2020

More Animals of Lockdown

Seagull Graffiti on the Barbican

Stanley – Ian Carroll's dog enjoying the solitude…

…and we said goodbye to the wooden animals in New George Street

All The UK's Biggest Festivals Were Cancelled

Not Just Another Day

It's not just another day, in a world full of chaos,
where life as we know has stumbled, and these times are sent to try us.

It's not just another day, when friends and family connect,

Through the power of social media, through love life and respect

It's not just another day, the planet it is healing;
Our air supply is cleaner, as we understand its meaning.

It's not just another day, as we fight to stay alive,
Human spirit as one, these days will soon subside.

It's not just another day, it's one step closer to the goal,

As loved ones come and go, and truths are all but told.
This world in which we live in, its course is set to heal,
All in the name of humanity, and all in the way that we feel.

We as humans have learnt, live for what is true,
At the end of these darkened days,
A beautiful world for us to view.

Paddy 1.5.20

Services Rendered

These bravest souls, who fight the fight,
From hospital wards, through dead of night,
We clap our hands to show our voice,
We praise you all, through hardest choice.

The war has started, the guns are out,
We keep our hands away from mouth,
You're masks are on, relentless love,
Saving lives, as everyone should.
Doctors, nurses, and carers thrive,
Tirelessly working, to keep us alive.

You put yourselves in firing line,
This wretched disease as people dying.
The NHS our saving grace,
Helping all, to win this race
Ambulance, stretchers, beds are full,
Together as one, we all must pull.
Join our hands our love shines through,
The NHS for me and you.

Paddy 27.03.20

The Barbican During Lockdown

Lunchtime on a sunny Sunday afternoon and there are very few people around; a time like this has never been seen before or hopefully will never be seen ever again…

Peaceful and silent, the once thriving Barbican is empty

Southside Street on the Barbican, usually busy – especially at 1:30pm on a Sunday afternoon - and only one person can be seen on the street and it was like this for months, as it turned into a ghostly shadow of its former self.

Free waters for runners on the Barbican showing the kindness of strangers and pasties still available, but no one to share them with.

"My personal experience of lockdown 2020 was one that started the Sunday before the official lockdown began on 23rd March.

The Sunday before I became ill, having COVID-19 type symptoms (not having had a test so will never be 100% sure) I have had flu once before but this truly knocked me for 6. I also carried what I've later learned is being dubbed post Covid syndrome for weeks after.

I was lucky to recover well without any medical care needed.

I was blown away by offers of help from our neighbours.

I was lucky to return to my keyworker role quickly.

I have loved seeing Plymouth businesses helping the wider community and seeing their innovation in keeping their businesses operational."

Aimee De Van (Plymouth)

"Couple of years ago I moved from a large detached house with no neighbours to a small terraced house in Plymouth.

My spare time was initially taken up in turning an unloved muddy back yard into a green and colourful garden - with more than a nod given to the old style garden with tin buckets, large galvanised steel planters and metal watering cans as I love that old cottage style and informal planting type of garden.

A few months before the pandemic I was in Exeter and decided to pop into a favourite haunt - a reclamation yard on a business estate around the Marsh Barton area. I was pleased to find an old wooden stepladder and purchased it as I planned to tie it to the front garden fence and stack terracotta pots filled with flowering plants on it.

In the pandemic my step ladder was cheery and neighbours passing by would comment from afar on how lovely it looked.

The ladder was there only a matter of weeks before someone walked down the path to my house and, shouting through my kitchen widow, called

"I don't want to come in. Do you want to sell your ladder ... I'll give you 15 quid for it!"

Despite my initial reluctance to enter into much of a conversation through my kitchen window with someone I didn't know, the chap persisted, told me his name was Greg, that he lived across the way and that his wife wanted my ladder as she'd seen it and loved it. Greg kept telling me that my old ladder is 'retro' and that his wife wanted to put pots on it. It struck me that Greg seemed oblivious to the fact I liked my old ladder purely because of its retro charm and that I was using it for exactly the same purpose as his wife wanted it for.

Insistent, Greg quickly upped his offer to £20 but I felt I needed to tell Greg that I had no intention of selling it because not only did I like the ladder but I'd bought it in a reclamation yard and I'd paid a bit for it. Clearly Greg found this response questionable.

"Oh, really? ... From a reclamation yard was it?"

And when I confirmed that I had bought it in Exeter Greg, coming closer to the kitchen window, exclaimed

"Well I'm not going to be able to drive all the way to Exeter... It's a long way and there's a pandemic!"

I had to laugh, I really thought Greg was being funny but he remained straight-faced and still wouldn't give up. He upped his offer to £25 whilst, still at my kitchen window, confided he had seen these old retro ladders on Marketplace and they went for £35 apparently but he hadn't managed to bag one. I sympathised with his predicament but wondered why Greg seemed to think I was running a retro ladder shop from my kitchen window!

The upshot? Well I let 'Greg from over the way' have the ladder purely for his cheek, he had more front than Brighton and I'd found the whole episode quite funny!

He clearly felt he couldn't go back to his wife without a deal having been struck. In the end I got given a bit more than the price I had paid for it so it was a win - win situation as it turned out.

I only hope Greg's wife does indeed love it as much as Greg was prepared to fight for it and it hasn't turned out to be a retro regret.

I'm now looking forward to finding another garden 'item' once lockdown is fully over but this time I'll stick whatever it happens to be in the back garden just to prevent any future browsers from haggling for items they might take a shine to.

Still, I must be the only person in lockdown who can make a profit from selling old lovable tat through their kitchen window without even trying!"

Debbie Charlick (Plymouth)

"Well, although we were in 'Lock-Down', I didn't really feel alone I still attended work everyday using Public Transport.
Knowing I was helping people kept me going, and seeing my friends and colleagues at work.
Living alone, work was my saviour.
However I have missed being able to do things with my Gran, my friends outside of work and the small things that make you feel good like Nails and Hair.
I can wait to go for meal out and not have to follow a one way system in the not too distance future."
Jennifer Bishop (Plymouth)

"One of the memories I will have with my husband in lockdown, is where we live in Yealmpton (a village just outside Plymouth) was the real community spirit that everyone had, especially at a time when we couldn't see family or friends.
We had over 125 volunteers and made most contact by Facebook.
V.E. Day was a big celebration, with everyone out in their gardens and displaying the Union Jack. The local Volunteer pub delivered hot meals and beer, and the village shop supplied nearly all that was needed. We even had social distancing nights in the garden (food from the pub and drinks) with our neighbours.
The garden looks great too.
So apart from missing our wonderful family to hug, this Village was buzzing.
Think we could get used to this."
Andrea Avery (Yealmpton nr. Plymouth)

Ok - lockdown in the Francis household, Plympton consisted of us redecorating our sitting room & plenty of decluttering.
Thankfully the sunny weather meant many hours in the garden, painting & planting while enjoying plenty of BBQ's & beers.
Celebrating VE Day with neighbours.
As key workers, we worked throughout following newly implemented social distancing rules.
Missing our & friends during lockdown proved the hardest thing but grateful that everyone remained safe & well.
As a way of keeping in touch, we have weekly quiz night via Zoom, which we are keeping going. The positive thing during lockdown has been to take life a little easier & enjoy our surroundings. It's been lovely to feel clean air, have less cars on the roads and enjoy outside exercise."
Rose Francis (Plymouth)

"I was furloughed for 9 weeks...
Sorted out my music collection and caught up with some classic Will Hay
films.
All in all, had a great time and would do it all again, although let's hope
the opportunity doesn't arise."
Andy Harris (Plymouth)

"Just thought you might be interested in this story about our mum, Violet,
who is 93 years old.
She has lived in a residential home for about a year after it became
dangerous for her to live on her own. She is very happy there and all her
family have visited everyday since she has been there (we work out a rota
on a Sunday for the week).
When lockdown happened it was understandable, but made it so difficult
for us all to maintain that closeness we had as a family.
Mum is very deaf and unless her hearing aids are working it's very hard
for us to talk.
The 'home' have been very good but it has been difficult to maintain our
close relationship.
She even had a third great grandchild born who she couldn't see!
When we heard that a Carer and a resident at the home had died from
COVID, we were devastated.
Our mum/gran/aunty/sister was at a greater risk than most and we had to
put our faith in the home to keep her safe!
Thankfully, they did a brilliant job, and all were safe in there, they'd kept
the beast at bay, only for us to learn a few weeks later, she had had a fall
and broken her leg after a fall at night.
We could not see her, talk to her, cuddle her and say everything was
going to be okay because of this horrible virus.
Again, more worry and stress while she was in hospital but yet again the
staff were brilliant and a week later she was back at the home.
We have been able to see her in the garden at the home now for a couple
of weeks, and amazingly she walked out with her frame!
We can't kiss and cuddle her, but can admire this lady for her strength,
determination and her refusal to leave us yet.
There is something about her generation that makes them very special."
Anne Kitchenham (Plymouth)

2020, the year we couldn't go to the seaside, so I brought it to our
garden!
Great fun painting my own archive for Covid-19."
Heather Hayne (Plymouth)

"We discovered some wonderful walks local to us that we had never been on. First family day out in 8 weeks was to Fernworthy.
We enjoyed being at home and lots of gardening!"
Kerry Taylor (Plymouth)

The Future is Key

Staying strong, in this giving light, pushing forward, keep up the fight,
The only way to conquer all is to believe in faith as we stand tall.
Harmony rises, through all that is made, in fields of dreams, the future is paved,
Lay darkest fears to rest at last, these darkened times, are soon to pass.

Closed eyes reveal what's deep inside, a beating heart, we all survive,
To live this life, on pastures new, as brighter day's for us to view.
Silenced voice for all to hear, we the people see things clear,
Fresh winds they blow, rejoice relive, as once again the joy to give.

Smiling eyes that once lay sullen, springs to life, the past that was stolen,
For now is the time to breathe this air, and fill our lungs, with futures care.
Paused still repeat what once it was, unto this life without just cause,
No more the sorrow shall render hearts beat, for this day is new, and we shall defeat.

So take deep breaths, let pure course through, in all of life, in all that we do,
For we are strong, and we will survive, in uncertain worlds we all feel alive.
Dream your dreams, and make them come through, smile your smile, in all that you do,
Love is the key, its faultless divine, till once again, in arms you are mine.

Paddy 2.04.20

Glenholt
'Community Good Neighbour Scheme'

"Glenholt Community Hub has been up and running now for nearly 2 years, as a means to bring 2 communities together socially whilst raising funds for our 'Glenholt Heartbeat Defibrillator Appeal Fund' which will see defibrillators in our community.

This has all been running quite successfully by means of monthly coach trips, community forum, swap shop, and weekly off key singing groups along with other events planned such as our 'Mayflower 400 Fancy Dress Street Party' which unfortunately has now had to be postponed until a later date due to the covid-19 pandemic we now find ourselves in.

In order to do all of this we regularly advertise through newsletters, posters & flyers on notice boards in Glenholt & the George Park & Ride Office, St Anne's Church & our local shops here in Glenholt, Southway public library, Social media facebook groups and the next door app.

Early in March it was becoming more apparent to us that there would be a huge need for some kind of community group here in Glenholt, that could help the most vulnerable and elderly in our community.

*So **"Glenholt Community Good Neighbour Scheme'** was set up and in action by 20th March 2020.*

In order to set this up, we produced a Covid-19 newsletter that we distributed throughout the whole of Glenholt & Glenholt Park, a total of over 900 homes in receipt of a copy. This newsletter outlined the seriousness of Covid-19, asked for help in the form of volunteers and gave guidance to all residents on what to do if help was needed.

My husband & I set ourselves up as co-ordinator's, to enable residents to call us and request help, we also saw over 50 volunteers coming forward with an offer of help.

Our main aim was to cover the whole of Glenholt with shopping, newspaper deliveries, prescriptions, dog walking, posting letters etc. or arrange a call from one of our compassionate befriending volunteers to chat to if any of our residents who are feeling really lonely or feeling down and really isolated due to living on their own.

*1. **Who is eligible** – all vulnerable residents shielding who are unable to leave their homes, whether in voluntary self isolation, chronic health issues, suffering from immune deficiency or at present are* suffering with the Covid-19 and find themselves or the whole family in isolation.

2.   **On average we receive 1 – 6 calls** with various requests for help a day, with our scheme now up and running for just over 17 weeks, we have dealt with many a call and helped so many local residents in need of our assistance.

3.   **Our aim and main area of cover** is the whole of Glenholt, however we have deviated from this when we have found families with no one else to turn to, either family members have made contact with us or social services.

4.   **Without speaking to all our volunteers** who we totally rely on, we have no wish to expand out any further in covering a wider area but are quite happy to remain as we are. At present we have a very successful system in place, with around 20 very reliable and active volunteers, some we have lost due to their own work or family commitments. We also have our very own chronic health issues to deal with on a daily basis, which renders us both on the shielding long-term list of people in total isolation.

5.   **We may need to take on a few more volunteers** at some point if the increase in volume of residents needing our help should increase at any time in the near future.

6.   **Our own referral service** is by means of newsletter, flyers, posters, social media, word of mouth, our very own volunteers looking out for residents, other family members checking out the Plymouth Good Neighbour Scheme (Caring for Plymouth) or Plymouth Labour Community Action Group. Once Plymouth Labour Community Action Group & PCC Caring for Plymouth were formed and up and running we saw an opportunity of registering and coming together and working as one under their umbrella and network, whilst still running very independently on our own. We are registered with our local (Londis) shop/Post Office, where we have managed to set up a scheme where residents can call the shop, place an order for some groceries and one of our volunteers will collect & deliver. Through our local shop we have also set – up 2 newspaper daily delivery rounds, having 2 of our youngest volunteers delivering newspapers, to approx 17 customers. Also working with Tesco at Roborough and having one of their home delivery managers help us set up originally a delivery service, they also are in receipt of a full list of our volunteers which helped immensely especially in the early days to save queuing. Tesco pharmacy is also working with us and one of the staff helping deliver prescriptions on her way home

from work for us. We do use other supermarkets and pharmacies in our local area to collect from and deliver but have found Tesco and our local Londis Store to be the most helpful in accommodating our volunteers and our services.

The greatest thing that has come out of all the pandemic for us is that, we have managed to support several elderly vulnerable residents along with helping those shielding due to ill health.

We have a great team of volunteers support and help from various other organisations and our local shops all coming together for the good of our neighbours. Without all of this there would have been more elderly being out and about, possibly picking up this virus and helping the spread. Instead what we have are some lovely residents truly appreciative to all of us especially our volunteers for all their help.

Where do we go from here as we enter Phase 2?

Well to be perfectly honest we can't see much changing within our group apart from us losing a few volunteers with going back to work. Our intention is to run our services for as long as needed. These volunteers are our very own 'unsung heroes' as far as we are concerned.

Of course in every area there appears to be those that must think the virus is not going to get them and are continuing to mix and form get-togethers regardless of government guidelines and rulings. Those that continue to go to the beaches and form crowds and those whom have been protesting all under some illusion, which only puts the one's shielding like ourselves determined not to come out of isolation until we know what damage these folk are causing.

There has been some lovely things coming out of Covid-19, in bringing communities together, our wildlife and mammals and our plants all thriving due to the lack of pollution and activity.

There are times everyday when I am rendered unfit to carry out any task due to my chronic illnesses but with us just co-ordinating we are able to take the calls, log all our callers and have a little chat with the residents who at times do feel very isolated or lonely before passing on their request through our 'What's App Group of Volunteers'.

17 weeks and counting now, hopefully we shall emerge at some point in the near future from our isolation or will we?

One of the interesting things I have learnt is that more emphasis needs to be put on supporting the elderly and disabled in our communities at all times not just through a pandemic."

Denise Mills (Plymouth)

Empty streets and children's Rainbow drawings…

Unlike many pubs, the Bread & Roses on Ebrington Street will not be opening its doors to the general public once more until early to mid August, due to the size and the difficulties of 'Social Distancing'.

The **NHS** were appreciated everywhere for the outstanding and exemplary work that they provided throughout the 'pandemic'.

All the local Public Houses were closed from March; this will not be the case from 4th July when they re-open once more, but with strict guidelines set in place to be followed…

Black 'crosses' began to appear on pavements outside shops everywhere to make sure that everyone stood 2 metres apart when queuing to enter many shops all over the city.

The closed up shops, the abandoned pubs, the empty streets with graffiti - Plymouth's Mutley Plain was starting to resemble a ghost town as the days turned into weeks and then further developed into months as the 'Lock-Down' took a stranglehold on the city…

Empty Shops Once More

When is a Mall not a Mall?
When it's a Mausoleum to shopping…

The Mall in all its empty glory

'Covid-19 Keep Apart' signs
appeared on the pavements
all over the City Centre

Read the Signs

Signs went up everywhere.

From reminders of where we could go, to washing our hands, the most popular being re 'social distancing' of 2m and thanks to 'Keyworkers'…

So many warnings, so many new rules to follow…

'Obey the RULES...'

From posters in coffee shops to signs fixed to park entrances, there were new rules everywhere and the majority of the public followed them, only the minority thought that they were above the 'new laws'.

The NHS staff and all other keyworkers were kept in high regard, with thanks everywhere, from the window signs to the 'Clap for Carers' which took place every Thursday evening at 8pm, where people would stand outside their homes and clap – showing their appreciation for the exemplary services that all these 'keyworkers' were providing, more than ever.

The Barcode was closed and the parks had new guidelines

Random message, not necessarily COVID-19 related

We Loved to Queue....

Being British, we queued. We waited patiently at shops – where the amount of people shopping was always limited. We queued to buy items, to only find out on reaching the inside of the store that they were out of stock that day due to 'binge buying'.
We queued for toilet rolls during the days of the BRP (Bog Roll Panic) and then a few weeks in the rationing ended and a new sense of normality began to prevail.

COVID-19 Panic Buying

Who remembers the early days before 'Lock-Down' took place?
Before everything in the shops went back to near normal, we panic buying fiasco. People swooped on supermarkets 'en masse' and purchased so much they didn't need.

People were greedy, people went over the top…

The lack of flour, the nonexistence of pasta and worst of all the over the top purchasing of toilet rolls!!
It was like getting a Willy Wonka style '*Golden Ticket*' when you went into a supermarket and they had toilet roll for sale, even if it was only a solitary 4-pack. Seeing people leave the supermarkets with two or three 24-packs of toilet roll was a common occurrence and why? People seemed to think that they wouldn't be allowed out of their homes for weeks, but as we know, it never got to be anything like that.

Empty shelves, empty larders, empty stomachs…

"So it's been a while, 30 years I doubt it will be 30 more.
I remember the '70s and '80s but I will admit I cried like a baby tonight.
So, much better than the rest of this year. YNWA.
I've been bored shirtless the rest of lockdown. I'm normally bored but it's
worse recently I've even considered getting a job!!!"
Yvonne Lovering (Plymouth)

"In a vain effort to stay fit during lockdown and to take advantage of the
good weather, I decided to go for a run on a Thursday evening.
After a couple of miles, I bumped into a friend so I stopped and had a
politically correct socially distanced chat for a few minutes. After 20
minutes I started again, but ran into another mate a few miles later to
stopped for another catch up.
By this stage I was literally running late although not actually aware of
the time, so I headed back.
As I approached home, my neighbours were out in force for the weekly
'Clap for Carers' celebration and much to my embarrassment clapped,
banged pans and cheered 'encouragement' to me as I ran down their
streets as if I was winning the London Marathon.
Mortifying.
I started running in the mornings!"
Gary Martin (Plymouth)

"The band Blue are the 'Nostradamus' of our generation.
They "got the city on lockdown" in 2006.
Just no one listened..."
Steve Clarke (Plymouth)

"My lockdown has been a very busy time with work, but also a time of learning too.

Learning how to teach hundreds of students online and manoeuvring a whole load of anxious people through new ways of working whilst trying to keep on top of all the other spinning plates.

Learning how to do a shop for around four to six different people, and how to navigate social distancing with other shoppers who don't understand what distance actually means.

Learning how to make bread.

Learning how to bake chocolate chip cookies.

Learning I need to ease back on baking chocolate chip cookies. Or at least on eating them.

Learning how to remember how good some friends are, when they go out of their way to get you flour when you post a joke on Facebook about all the shops not having any, thus enabling the baking of more cookies.

I've learned to spend less and less time on social media after seeing the worst of people coming out at a time when we should be seeing the best of us.

During lockdown I've also found myself constantly writing. Thoughts of sorts, songs, micro essays, poems, and lectures. Writing about the lockdown, about social and moral issues, about statues, and about education in a time of crisis.

I had a commission from The Box – 'State of Emergency' - writing a walk (with a friend, in a wholly Internet based collaboration) for people to take that explores ego and love in the city of Plymouth.

Lockdown has been hard.

I miss my family and friends. But it has also given us all a chance to see what we are made of, and to learn a little bit more about ourselves."

Jason Hirons (Plymouth)

"Who would have thought 6 months ago that we'd all be searching for hours online for a nice reusable face mask, panic buying toilet roll and pasta or quickly shuffling in the opposite direction if a stranger comes within 6 foot!

The worrying thing is this all feels strangely normal and acceptable already."

Donna Wilson (Plymouth)

"My main memory is seeing the traffic disappear overnight and the streets being deserted.

Slowly but surely as lockdown eased, traffic appeared along with more people."

Colin Sherman (Plymouth)

"One of the most surreal experiences ever!
An emotional roller coaster ride, a feeling of upheaval on an immense
scale.
I'd recently moved to a new home, on the Rame peninsular in Cornwall,
prior to the covid outbreak. (Lots of work in the garden to do, finding my
feet etc.)
My daughter had just moved into her own flat - but in Notts.
The calling to be closer to family during the lockdown was immense. So I
packed very randomly, emptied my freezer and was taken up Notts on the
20/03 by my son we had a quick pint in the d n c and that was the last pint
in pub to this day.
Still haven't been on public transport.
To sum up scary times with memories of my daughter taking the p••s out
of me, too much time for tiktok.
And a covid pod..."
Jane Spencer (Millbrook nr. Plymouth)

"I am soooo boring, with no life, that 'lockdown' has
been no different to my normality really."
Colleen Spencer (Plymouth)

"Lock down' for me has been great!
Have enjoyed the traffic free journeys to work, quality time with the family and the slower pace of life!
Long may it continue!
But on a negative side I have really missed my family and friends who we have not been able to get close to because of the social distancing...
Oh and I don't like queuing!!"
Nicola Lamerton (Tavistock nr. Plymouth)

"My lockdown experience is driving my bus in & around town being a ghost town and seeing only key workers like you (Ian Carroll) walking to & from work and you waiting for the bus - as you missed one by 5 minutes, me beeping my horn at you too."
Chris Adams (Plymouth)

"To be honest, I've still been working through it same as you I'm guessing.
It's certainly been weird and the lack of gigs is shit, but I'm quite happy to keep socially distancing, as I've always done."
Daniel Southwould (Plymouth)

"I missed and still miss my commute to work and to have some routine in my day.

Initially would 'walk to work' would go to Beaumont park and back, the dog now puts his feet firmly on the ground and won't walk that far now before 8am.

The wedding was planned for 25th April. In March I was still convinced it would go ahead, family would arrive from Australia and we would have a big celebration, Boris took the decision away from us with lockdown. On the day of the wedding we walked to the venue had a drink outside - still all seems a bit surreal.

Also go for a bike ride every morning at 6am, gradually the traffic increased, but seeing the same people out walking."

Tracie Mansell (Plymouth)

"As many people know throughout my life I have had a distinct fear of germs. So following the lockdown announcement lots of people have asked me –

"How are you dealing with this virus pandemic?" to which my reply has been "absolutely fine actually as I have been planning for this moment for years".

In fact in a lot of ways I am quite enjoying it, handshakes are no more (never actually saw the point in them), at restaurants I no longer feel I am sat on the laps of the couple next to me as the tables are all now 2 metres apart and my particular favourite is that those 'space invaders' in my office now have to stay behind the clearly marked red/white hazard tape I have deployed on the floor.

Isn't it funny that we are now discussing things that we would never have before such as:

"Ooooh that's a nice face mask, where did you get that one from?"

"Have you been staying alert?" and who can forget the good old

"Do you want to be in my bubble?"

Businesses up and down the country are now cashing in on making hand gel. Looking in my drawer I am currently stocked up on Cussons Carex Moisture hand gel, Boots Aloe Vera hand cleansing gel and oh look Carex also have their 'Original Complete Defence hand gel.

If only I took out shares in Carex?

Weird to think that all our lives have changed due to a tiny bat in China. My life has definitely changed, more often than not I am now riding my bike to work and back home again. Really love the moment when I am peddling my heart out up a hill and someone with an electric bike hits their power boost button and motors on past me... I feel like shouting "Yeah thanks for that, but you're cheating!" but I choose not to as by then I am massively out of breath and would worry what they would do to me if they turned around!

The days I do not ride my bike I have braved the DREADED bus. But it's been ok as I have my super hero facemask to protect me. But wearing a facemask is not a great look when you have glasses.

Take me for instance; I often have to sprint for the bus, as I am often late for it. Once I get to the bus I then put my facemask on which in turn fogs up my glasses due to the fact I am panting for dear life. I then have the fun task of navigating my way on to the bus by touch and scent alone and out of the corner of my fogged up glasses I can see all the other passengers trying not to laugh.

What a great way to start the day!"

Olle Putt (Plymouth)

Food During Lockdown

Staple dietary needs were still met during 'Lockdown'…

Even dogs have nutritional food needs during
the Lockdown, even if they are made of cloth and squeak…

"From the age of 17 when I first went to the Van Dike, over the ferry from Torpoint - walk up the hill to the club to see such amazing bands.
I have always loved watching local bands and there are some great ones around, that's what I miss now.
The live music gives me such a buzz, makes you feel alive instead of just existing.
Bring back the bands. Maybe bandstands in the park?"
Julie Norman (Plymouth)

'Many a true word, spoken in graffiti…'

'A once empty road,
Complete lack of running feet
Silence rules the street' – Anon

A solitary tree braves the oncoming storms
and the chaos of COVID-19

Graffiti During Lockdown

Graffiti sprung up all over the walls during 'Lock-Down' – some old, some new, some amazing, some scrawled…

Even the City Centre signs didn't escape the 'tagging'…

Empty – greatly missed 'outlets' – were daubed lovingly with graffiti, reminding us how we missed them.

Random Graffiti in Mutley

'Eat More Greens'

The 'Lockdown' at Night

Unlike any other time - in most of lives - we were enveloped in a deathly, all encompassing silence.

Taking my dog out for his final walk of the day –usually still noisy with cars, sirens and people – I was met each evening with nothing.

It was like being on the moon. The city had lost all of its atmosphere and with it, any sounds that we are all accustomed to.

The ambience was totally different and now that places are starting to open back up, I miss those days of quietness.

Flickering street lights, but
nothing much else…

No people, no cars moving, the only company on the streets were the buzz of the overhead electric streetlights.

Not busy at all at 9:30pm of a Summer's evening

More Early Days...

Parked cars, going nowhere,
planted trees, leaves shed…

Masks on Public Transport

*From **Monday 15th June** it became compulsory to wear a face mask on all public transport – buses, trains, trams etc. – unless you fell into one of the 'exemption groups', asthmatics, emphysema etc. There were many designs and a variety of masks available and more became available by the day.*

The Shops Were Closed

From a thriving, busy City Centre, to an empty shell of what was once a shopping mecca for the people of Plymouth and the nearby areas – it was just silent…

Saturday afternoon and it's all quiet in New George Street

'Empty staircases, leading nowhere. Where once there were crowds of happy shoppers, now lies the dust of forgotten hope…'

The 'New Look' Socially distanced Cap'n
Jaspers on the Barbican

Together We Are Stronger

Bow down in this time of crisis, and pray in this time of need,
Together we are all now the sufferings, our families we're all try to feed.
This ignorance will soon be the death, of all that who choose to resist,
As bodies throughout all the countries, lay victim as this virus persists.

This world that we know of is changing, the faces of friends far and wide,
Together we brave isolation, in rooms where we're all meant to hide.
But people they fail to realise, how selfish and cruel they can be,
Out walking in fresh air and sunshine, no distance between family.

Take heed of all of the warnings, instructions and rule we must follow,
Stay safe in your own little hideout, and live through to the birth of tomorrow.
No gatherings, no contact, no shindigs, in this boat we are all in together,
To fight the fight we as humans, shall battle this stormy weather.

It's not hard, it's not difficult, nor rocket science, we must all take notes of and learn,
In this, a time of pure crisis, stand strong, let's ease this concern.
Our brothers, our fathers, our sisters, together as one we are stronger,
Please follow what we are all meant to do, and look back in the future and ponder.

Paddy 23.03.20

The Barbican is Closed...

As the months passed by, the Barbican in Plymouth became quieter and quieter, starting to resemble a 'ghost town' minus the tumbleweeds...

Empty cobbles = peaceful times for residents...

Even the busy times, just weren't – a once heaving
South Side Street is so quiet you could hear a
seagull at 200 yards.

The only sounds on the Barbican was the wind catching the chimes on the boats and slapping the rigging against the masts.

The once busy area between the Three Crowns and the Maritime public houses was empty and 'DEAD'…

When will it all be back to normal once more?

TALKING TO YOURSELF
(SLIGHT LANCASHIRE ACCENT)

WHEN I WAS A LAD
TALKING TO YOURSELF
WAS CONSIDERED BAD

IF YOU KEPT IT UP
THEY PUT YOU AWAY
IN A BLOODY GREAT PLACE
WHERE YOU HAD TO STAY

BUT NOW YOU SEE THEM
EVERY DAY
STROLLING ALONG
AND PRATTELING AWAY

THEY TELL YOU OF THE WEATHER
THEY TELL YOU WHERE THEY ARE
THEY SAY THEY'RE GETTING ON THE BUS
OR GOING TO THE CAR

THEY TELL YOU MUM'S GOT HEAMORROIDS
OR DAD IS OFF HIS ROCKER
OR ELSE I'VE MET A TASTY LASS
WITH A LOVELY PAIR OF KNOCKERS

YOU CAN RECOGNISE THEM EASILY
BY WIRES HANGING FROM THEIR EARS
AND A DISTURBING, SERIOUS, CANDOUR
I TELL YOU, IT'S VERY QUEER

IT MAKES ME WONDER, SOMETIMES
IF I'VE GONE AND LOST THE PLOT
WHY I HANG ON, AND GO ON LIVING
WITH THIS CRAZY BLOODY LOT

MET, MAY 2020

"This is just a little personal snapshot of my lockdown experience.
COVID-19 became very real to me on Friday the 13th of March. My two
sons and I were at Bristol Airport about to fly to Dublin for my niece's
wedding, which was the following day.

My younger son Fintan was to fly home two days later to rehearse for his
part in 'Our House' with Plymkids - due to be performed that week at the
Athenaeum Theatre.

My eldest son, Cian, and I would fly home on the 18th of March so we
could enjoy an authentic St Patrick's Day celebration in Dublin with our
Irish family members.

Not long after we arrived at the airport, we received two texts: one to say
that the wedding had been postponed and the other to say that the show
had been postponed.

Both were put off due to the risk of COVID-19.

Over the next few weeks, life as we knew it changed beyond
recognition. There were desperate shopping missions – it took me 3 days
and many store visits to get a loaf of bread! Toilet roll? Forget it! Some
supermarkets were limiting the purchase of essential items.

BEVERLEY KINSELLA

You need your wits about you too, to make sure you correctly follow all
the arrows without upsetting anyone! Carrying a bottle of hand sanitiser
is essential, but carrying cash is becoming a thing of the past; contactless

payments are preferred and actually essential in some stores; a quick nip to the shop doesn't exist anymore. We need to be prepared to queue to enter, follow the one-way system and to stay 2 metres apart at all times. Non-essential stores opened recently.

My iPhone needed a repair, so I booked an appointment at the Apple Store in Drake Circus. When I arrived, I had to check-in with Apple staff outside the mall, have my temperature taken and answer some questions. Luckily, I passed this interview and was presented with a mask to wear in the store.

Fintan's life has been the most affected.

On Wednesday 18th March, after Boris Johnson announced that schools had to close by that Friday, I received a text advising us that Fintan's school, DHSB, had closed that day. Fintan is in year 13, the final year of studying 'A' levels. That Wednesday was his last ever day of school and we weren't aware of until it was over.

Sadly, there was no time or opportunity for goodbyes or thank-you's, nor the traditional and obligatory 'last morning of school' photo.

In the days that followed, we learned that Fintan's 'A' level exams had been cancelled, as had his prom.

Also, he was in the process of auditioning for drama schools, and the auditions were subsequently moved online. Fintan started working at Morrison's in 2018, but since finishing school he has worked nearly every day to help out, doing an amazing job, like all of our key workers. I am very proud of him.

Rain wasn't going to stop play for Fintan's 18th birthday though. Obviously, our original plan to go to London went out the window, as did Plan B, namely the pub.

Luckily, there was a Plan C: Fintan is partial to Roam, a local microbrewery and taproom in Peverell. As visiting Roam was off the cards, I created Hoam in our garden, with custom glasses, coasters and a t-shirt to boot. Thankfully there was good weather all day, and his friends visited in shifts, helping him to narrowly avoid a locked down 18th with no one but his mum!

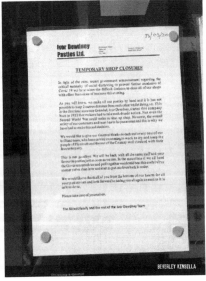

On the 23rd of March, I admit that when Ivor Dewdney's announced that they were closing due to the pandemic, I rushed to Stoke to panic buy pasties – one to eat that day and emergency ones in the freezer which actually survived until the 29th June!

When the pandemic started, we had to get used to new words and phrases such as herd immunity, social distancing and furlough, as well as singing Happy Birthday twice whilst washing our hands. That all seems a lifetime ago now.

I'd also never heard of Zoom – now I'm a regular participant, although I have to sit in my car at the top of my cul-de-sac to get a good signal. I've had Zoom meetings with friends, the school PTFA, cast members of a TV show, cast members of one of my favourite musicals and with members of my favourite band. I had to pay for some but those were for charity, so win-win!

Fintan has even managed to continue his rehearsals through Zoom for the 3 shows he is involved in. The show must go on! As yet there are no new dates for the performances.

Our lockdown celebrations have evolved from Mother's Day on the 22nd March – I stood outside my mum and dad's closed patio doors, holding up 3 sheets of paper saying 'Happy Mother's Day' – to Father's Day on the 21st June, when we were able to enjoy a socially distanced get together on my parents' patio. It was a lovely afternoon, which was appreciated all the more for what we have been through, although rain did curtail our celebration a bit.

For most of the lockdown we were blessed with fantastic weather, which made it more bearable. It also allowed us to have a socially distanced VE Day 75 street party, on which the sun was shining all day, ensuring a good time for all. One of my lovely neighbours was telling us about being taken on The Hoe on VE Day in 1945. Hearing first-hand memories was priceless.

We couldn't go anywhere for a while, which was a shame because the price of fuel dropped dramatically, and car parking charges were waived – as were the tolls for Tamar Bridge and Torpoint Ferry.

Personally, I have hugely missed going to the theatre.

Unfortunately, it seems like theatres will be the last to have restrictions lifted. I sincerely hope that they can survive the pandemic. Many theatre companies, including Andrew Lloyd Webber's, have streamed their productions online for us to enjoy at home. It's not the same but it was still fantastic. On the plus side, at least there were no security bag checks, no queues for the toilets and nobody with big hair fidgeting or crunching food in front of me all evening – every cloud has a silver lining!

During this time my eldest son Cian has been in Bristol, studying for his Masters. I had last seen him at Bristol Airport in March, but we were finally reunited on the 29th June, when I helped him move home. It was lovely to see him and belatedly give him his Easter Eggs.

Alas my lockdown to-do list is nowhere near completion, but tomorrow is another day.

Hair appointment is booked for the 8th July – can't wait! Next step is the battle of the lockdown bulge!

A big thank you to all our key workers out there, and remember to take care and keep safe!"

Beverley Kinsella (Plymouth)

Empty Streets, Empty Seats…

With the Lockdown in full effect, the Theatre Royal Plymouth closed its doors and that's the way that they have stayed for whole period and the foreseeable future.

However, on the 5th July the Government announced a £1.57 billion support for Britain's cultural, arts and heritage institutions, to try and save the closure of many theatres, music venue, cinemas and museums, hopefully this will be successful in saving them all.

Even More Early Days…

Cornwall Street just after 6pm

Empty streets with rubbish beginning to build up - from people spending time at home with takeaways, supermarket beers and just not going out.

"Lockdown, has brought so many different challenges to us all depending on our personal situations. One challenge was how to make my 84 year old mum have a meaningful birthday when she's been isolating since mid March, lives alone, with no family allowed to travel to see her.

I tried a few bakeries to see about having a cake delivered, with no joy. A Facebook plea was answered by a friend who delivered some cup cakes. How to make the day special?

Call the Police!

Mum was WPC in the '60s and I know there's a retired police association, which is supported by serving officers.

I contacted the Community Police Team who came up trumps with a birthday visit, a homemade cake and a lovely home made card. They tweeted about it and mum then had birthday wishes from all over!

She even ended up being interviewed by the BBC!

Thank you Plymouth Community Police Team for helping mum mark at least one day of lockdown as special.

It's not been easy, she's stuck to the rules and continues to social distance because of various health conditions, so she was feeling pretty fed up with her 4 walls and it made her day."

Vanessa Cook (Bristol)

A Lockdown Poem

I look through the window smiling faces is what I see.
Happy and smiling, looking at me.
Blowing me kisses and handprints on the windowpane.
I love seeing you, but it's not the same.
But for now we have to make do with this.
Until the day we can hug and kiss.
To hold each other once again.
Until then nothing will be the same.
But we are thankful we can see each other.
I love you all, your funny ol' Muzza.
XXXXX

Read the Signs

When places started to open once more, the signs and warnings came in full.

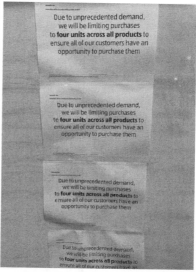

The posters on bus shelters, tempted us with food that we could not buy…

New 'anti-litter' signs went up after the Barbican fiasco prior to the pubs opening once more.

Sweet words and memories
to be rebuilt once more…

Messenger guards the front of
the Theatre Royal Plymouth

Printed in Great Britain
by Amazon